D0949118

THE END TIMES

To Martha —
Love & Blessings

John Van Auken

THE END TIMES

Prophecies of Coming Changes

Includes prophecies and predictions from

The Bible — Nostradamus
Holy Mother — Edgar Cayce

John Van Auken

ARE PRESS

**ASSOCIATION FOR
RESEARCH AND
ENLIGHTENMENT**

A.R.E. Press • Virginia Beach • Virginia

A.R.E. Press
215 67th Street
Virginia Beach, VA 23451-2061

Library of Congress Cataloging-in-Publication Data
Van Auken, John, 1946-
The end times : prophecies of coming changes / John Van
Auken.
    p. cm.
Originally published: Virginia Beach, Va. : Inner Vision
Pub. Co., 1994.
Includes bibliographical references (p. 167).
ISBN 0-87604-363-5 (trade paper)
1. Prophecies (Occultism). 2. End of the world. 3. Bible—
Prophecies—End of the world. 4. Cayce, Edgar, 1877-1945. 5.
Nostradamus, 1503-1566. 6. Mary, Blessed Virgin, Saint—Ap-
paritions and miracles. I. Title.
BF1791.V36 1996
133.3—dc20   96-21356

Contents

Introduction

Many speakers and writers in recent times have been expressing troubling ideas of coming major earth changes, everything from massive earthquakes to devastating pole shifts. I decided to investigate these ideas for my own edification. I was surprised to find many modern and ancient prophecies that did appear to forecast major changes for our little blue planet. Of all the sources for these prophecies, I found four that I thought represented the largest and best body of material: the Bible, Nostradamus (and with him I have included the works of Malachi and the Monk of Padua), apparitions of the Holy Mother of Jesus, and the great "sleeping prophet" Edgar Cayce.

However, when I got into the material more deeply, I found that few of the prophecies could be published without including the context in which they presented the earth changes. For example, as I studied the Bible, it became clear to me that an overarching theme ran from Genesis to The Revelation but was not commonly understood by most followers of biblical prophecies—including Jews, Christians, and Muslims, each of whom considers themselves to be the children of Abraham. I found it impossible to focus exclusively on earth-change prophecies without including the context or the background in which these changes were being presented.

This is not just a book about earth changes. It is about the "End Times," not the end of the world but the end of a long era or age and the beginning of a new one.

This is not a book about doom but about new hope after much needed change is accomplished.

However, it is not just a book of optimism or philosophy either. I've included all the hard news of serious physical changes to this earth, changes that are going to take many lives and affect many countries, continents, and oceans.

My intention is not to alarm people into living drastically different lifestyles, such as hoarding food and living in bunkers. My intention is to share what I've found about these prophecies, much of which is positive if we understand better who we really are and what life is really about.

John Van Auken
September 1996

1

The Prophecies of the Bible

Biblical prophecy has proved difficult to interpret. Some of the reasons for this are due to the imagery contained in them and an apparent purposefulness in obscuring their truth from the profane and the curious. The imagery in these prophecies comes from a deeper level of consciousness, thus requiring us to get into that level of consciousness before understanding is realized. Some of the messages are holistic, yet we strive to interpret them linearly. Some messages are dealing with the microcosm, but we strive to interpret them in the macrocosm. Nevertheless, the promise is:

> Ask and it will be given to you; seek and you

will find; knock and the door will be opened to
you. For everyone who asks receives; he who
seeks finds; and to him who knocks, the door
will be opened. (Matt. 7:7-8)

I have also found that the biblical stories and prophecies are difficult to understand if one doesn't first realize
that what we call "man" or humans were originally
"gods" or spirits. Here are two statements from the
Bible, Old and New Testaments, that bear witness to
this:

Ps. 82:6   I said, "You are gods; you are all sons
of the Most High."

John 10:34   Jesus answered them, "Is it not
written in your Law, 'I have said you are gods'?"

The children of God were created and lived in the
heavens, or in the consciousness of God, *before* they began to live in the flesh and the earth. This is important to
remember when trying to understand the predictions in
the scriptures.

There were *two* creations in Genesis. The first (Gen.
1:26-27) was when we were created in the image of God,
which is *spirit*—"God is Spirit" (John 4:24). Then, we
were created again (Gen. 2:5-7) from the dust of the
earth, or flesh. Now, there are two aspects to us, one
spirit or godly and the other flesh or human. Here are
those passages from Genesis:

Gen. 1:27   *So God created man in his own image, in the image of God he created him; male
and female he created them.*

Gen. 2:4-8   This is the account of the heavens

and the earth when they were created. When the Lord God made the earth and the heavens—and no shrub of the field had yet appeared on the earth and no plant of the field had yet sprung up, for the Lord God had not sent rain on the earth *and there was no man to work the ground,* but streams came up from the earth and watered the whole surface of the ground—*the Lord God formed the man from the dust of the ground and breathed into his nostrils the breath of life, and the man became a living being.*

Now the Lord God had planted a garden in the east, in Eden; and there he put the man he had formed.

Notice after we were created in Genesis 1 in the image of God (i.e., spirit), there was still "no man to work the ground." This was because we were not physical, not human, or in the flesh, yet. As the last line indicates, God had not "formed" the man yet. Then, a different level of God, called the *Lord God* (Yahweh Elohim) created us a second time, now in the flesh—"from the dust of the ground."

Later, the Lord God divides the man-woman into separate male and female beings. At this point in the creation story, we were still immortal beings that lived in direct contact with the Lord God.

When we keep in mind that each being is both a godling and a human—or in biblical terms, a "son/daughter of God" and a "son/daughter of man"—then we can better understand why the biblical stories and prophecies are the way they are.

THE CURSE

If one reads carefully, the *first* biblical prophecy is given by the Lord God to Adam and Eve as they leave the Garden and the presence of the Lord. At this point, the godlings had descended out of their heavenly consciousness, completely into physical consciousness and human bodies. This was not meant to be, but since they used their free wills to make it so, they had to go through it. In this next passage, the Lord God is speaking to our earthly selves. The Lord God does not want us to stay forever in the earth, and so He has cursed the earth, that it will not give us ultimate satisfaction and contentment.

> Gen. 3:14-19   So the Lord God said to the serpent, "Because you have done this, Cursed are you above all the livestock and all the wild animals! You will crawl on your belly and you will eat dust all the days of your life.
>
> "And I will put enmity between you and the woman, and between your offspring and her offspring; he [i.e., her offspring] will crush your head, and you will bruise his heel."
>
> To the woman he said, "I will greatly increase your pains in childbearing; with pain you will give birth to children. Your desire will be for your husband, and he will rule over you."
>
> To Adam he said, "Because you listened to your wife and ate from the tree about which I commanded you, 'You must not eat of it,' cursed is the ground because of you; through painful toil you will eat of it all the days of your life.
>
> "It will produce thorns and thistles for you, and you will eat the plants of the field.
>
> "By the sweat of your brow you will eat your

food until you return to the ground, since from it you were taken; for dust you are and to dust you will return."

Entry of the children of God into the physical world was not part of the great plan. But since the children chose the flesh over the spirit, they were then cursed to struggle through the realm of flesh until they chose the spirit and the realm of the Garden consciousness. Eventually, the woman would produce an offspring that would crush the serpent's head, even as its evil bruises the Messiah's heel. This prophecy of the Messiah is important, and will appear throughout the biblical prophecies. In the meantime, life in the earth will be hard for all concerned: serpent, woman, and man.

Gen. 3:21-24   The Lord God made garments of skin for Adam and Eve and clothed them.

And the Lord God said, "The man has now become like one of us, knowing good and evil. He must not be allowed to reach out his hand and take also from the Tree of Life and eat, and live forever."

So the Lord God banished him from the Garden of Eden to work the ground from which he had been taken.

After he drove the man out, he placed on the east side of the Garden of Eden cherubim and a flaming sword flashing back and forth to guard the way to the Tree of Life.

Now we, the celestial, immortal children of God, have become predominantly terrestrial and mortal. We no longer have access to the Tree of Life. That is, not until we reach the end of this great journey described in the last book of the Bible, *The Revelation*. Here we find that the Tree of Life has been given back to the children, who may eat from it freely, and may drink the water of life freely. The story is from the loss of the Garden in Genesis to the "new heaven" and "new earth" of the final chapters in Revelation:

Rev. 21:1-6 *Then I saw a new heaven and a new earth, for the first heaven and the first earth had passed away, and there was no longer any sea.*

I saw the Holy City, the new Jerusalem, coming down out of heaven from God, prepared as a bride beautifully dressed for her husband.

And I heard a loud voice from the throne saying, *"Now the dwelling of God is with men, and he will live with them. They will be his people, and God himself will be with them and be their God.*

"He will wipe every tear from their eyes. There will be no more death or mourning or crying or pain, for the old order of things has passed away."

He who was seated on the throne said, "I am making everything new!" Then he said, "Write this down, for these words are trustworthy and true."

He said to me: "It is done. I am the Alpha and the Omega, *the Beginning and the End.* To him who is thirsty I will give to drink freely from the spring of the Water of Life."

Rev. 22:1-5 Then the angel showed me *the River of the Water of Life,* as clear as crystal, flowing from the throne of God and of the Lamb down the middle of the great street of the city.

On each side of the river stood *the Tree of Life*, bearing twelve crops of fruit, yielding its fruit every month. *And the leaves of the Tree are for the healing of the nations.*

No longer will there be any curse. The throne of God and of the Lamb will be in the city, and his servants will serve him.

They will see his face, and his name will be on their foreheads.

There will be no more night. They will not need the light of a lamp or the light of the sun, for the Lord God will give them light. And they will reign for ever and ever.

Rev. 2:7   He who has an ear, let him hear what *the Spirit says . . .* To him who overcomes, *I will give the right to eat from the Tree of Life, which is in the paradise of God.*

Obviously, it all ends happily ever after.

Why is it so important to understand these elements of the Bible before we can understand the prophecies? Because the prophecies are all about the journey from the fall from Spirit and God's company, through the struggles with self-will and self-consciousness in the physical body and the earth, then back into the full consciousness and attunement with the Spirit and God.

Now, when the Lord condemns or purges the flesh or the earth, we understand that it is to make room for the Spirit, which is the true nature of every being. When the prophecies scream for an end to earth by fire, flood, plague, famine, and so on, we understand that it is a cry for the rebirth of the spirit by subduing the influences and demands of the flesh. Then, once the spirit is reborn, we unite these two aspects of ourselves in a "new heaven" and a "new earth." The curse is gone. All is new again. Every tear wiped away, and joy is full.

THE END TIMES' PROPHECIES

The first prophecy to use the term "End Times" is found in the book of the prophet Daniel. It is the angel Gabriel that uses the term.

> Dan. 8:15-19   While I, Daniel, was watching the vision and trying to understand it, there before me stood one who looked like a man.
>
> And I heard a man's voice from the Ulai [a river in Babylon] calling, "Gabriel, tell this man the meaning of the vision."
>
> As he came near the place where I was standing, I was terrified and fell prostrate. "Son of man," he said to me, "understand that the vision concerns *the time of the end.*"
>
> While he was speaking to me, I was in a deep sleep, with my face to the ground. Then he touched me and raised me to my feet.
>
> He said: "I am going to tell you what will happen later in the time of wrath, because the vision concerns the appointed *time of the end.*"

Clearly, Gabriel is saying that Daniel's vision is about "the time of the end." He goes on to tell Daniel just how long it will be until the end time.

> Dan. 7:25   He [the earthly ruler] will speak against the Most High and oppress his saints and try to change the set times and the laws. The saints will be handed over to him for a time, times and half a time.

We might ask, "Why are the saints handed over to the

earthly ruler for a time, times and half a time?" Remember, the flesh and the earth are now integral portions of our total being. We are the earthly ruler—both in our own bodies and out among the world. Therefore, God is allowing this newly acquired portion of our being to reign for a time, hoping that it will seek reunion with God rather than continue its self-seeking, earthly ways. But a time to end this matter has been set.

> Dan. 12:6-7   "How long will it be before these astonishing things are fulfilled?" The man clothed in linen, who was above the waters of the river, lifted his right hand and his left hand toward heaven, and I heard him swear by him who lives forever, saying, "It will be for *a time, times and half a time.* When the power of the holy people has been finally broken, all these things will be completed."

Why must the power of the "holy people" be broken before all these things are completed? Because in the Garden, we chose the flesh over the spirit, self-interests over God's interests. The penalty was loss of the spiritual, i.e., the holy, and to live in the cursed flesh/earth until we chose to rebirth the spirit and reunite with God. Stern? Yes. Cruel? Not if you consider that our present nature is an *acquired* one that limits ourselves and God's ability to communicate with us. Then, God's curse is holding a firm position to keep us from completely losing everything we were meant to be. As Jesus cried, "And now, Father, glorify me in your presence with the glory *I had with you before the world began.*" (John 17:5, my italics)

In Genesis we see the beginning of our duality in the two children that Adam and Eve conceived: Cain and Abel. In Hebrew, Cain literally means "acquired" and

Abel means "breath." The breath is what the Lord God gave us when he made us of the earth—"the breath of life." And, as is seen in the Genesis story, God loves Abel. But the acquired one, Cain, is not pleasing to God. Yet, when Cain confronts God over this, God replies: "If you do what is right, will you not be accepted? But if you do not do what is right, then sin is crouching at your door; it desires to have you, but you must master it." (Gen. 4:7)

As we will learn from the chapter on the Edgar Cayce prophecies, Cayce states that "the time, times and half-time" *are over*. This would mean, of course, that we are in the End Times. Here is what is prophesied.

Three sections of the Bible convey the major insights into the End Times: (1) Daniel's visions, (2) Jesus' teaching on the Mount of Olives, and (3) John's visions during the Revelation.

Since there is so much of it, repeated in slightly different ways in various books of the Bible, I will try to outline and highlight the key elements.

Let's begin with Daniel's visions and the Revelation's. Then, we'll look at Jesus' teaching on the Mount of Olives.

DANIEL & REVELATION

Daniel's First Dream/Vision

Dan. 7:1-18, 21-28   In the first year of Belshazzar, king of Babylon, Daniel had a dream, and visions passed through his mind as he was lying on his bed. He wrote down the substance of *his dream*.

Daniel said: "In my vision at night I looked, and there before me were the *four winds* of heaven churning up the great sea.

"*Four great beasts*, each different from the others, came up out of the sea.

"The first was like *a lion,* and it had the wings of an eagle. I watched until its wings were torn off and it was lifted from the ground so that it stood on two feet like a man, and the heart of a man was given to it.

"And there before me was a second beast, which looked like *a bear.* It was raised up on one of its sides, and it had three ribs in its mouth between its teeth. It was told, 'Get up and eat your fill of flesh!'

"After that, I looked, and there before me was another beast, one that looked like *a leopard.* And on its back it had four wings like those of a bird. This beast had four heads, and it was given authority to rule.

"After that, in my vision at night I looked, and there before me was a *fourth beast*—terrifying and frightening and very powerful. It had large iron teeth; it crushed and devoured its victims and trampled underfoot whatever was left. It was different from all the former beasts, and it had ten horns.

"While I was thinking about the horns, there before me was *another horn, a little one,* which came up among them; and *three of the first horns were uprooted* before it. *This horn had eyes like the eyes of a man and a mouth that spoke boastfully.*

"As I looked, thrones were set in place, and the Ancient of Days took his seat. His clothing was as white as snow; the hair of his head was white like wool. His throne was flaming with fire, and *its wheels were all ablaze.*

"*A river of fire* was flowing, coming out from before him. Thousands upon thousands attended him; ten thousand times ten thousand stood before him. The court was seated, and *the books were opened.*

"Then I continued to watch because of the boastful words the horn was speaking. I kept looking until the beast was slain and *its body destroyed and thrown into the blazing fire.*

(The other beasts had been stripped of their authority, *but were allowed to live for a period of time.*)

"In my vision at night I looked, and there before me was *one like a son of man,* coming with the clouds of heaven. He approached the Ancient of Days and was led into his presence.

"*He was given authority, glory and sovereign power; all peoples, nations and men of every language worshiped him. His dominion is an everlasting dominion that will not pass away, and his kingdom is one that will never be destroyed.*

"I, Daniel, was troubled in spirit, and the visions that passed through my mind disturbed me.

"I approached one of those standing there and asked him the true meaning of all this. So he told me and *gave me the interpretation* of these things:

" '*The four great beasts are four kingdoms that will rise from the earth.*

" '*But the saints of the Most High will receive the kingdom and will possess it forever—yes, for ever and ever*' . . .

"*As I watched, this horn* [i.e., the fourth beast] *was waging war against the saints and defeating them, until the Ancient of Days came and pronounced judgment in favor of the saints of the Most High, and the time came when they possessed the kingdom.*

"He gave me this explanation: *'The fourth beast is a fourth kingdom that will appear on earth. It will be different from all the other kingdoms and will devour the whole earth, trampling it down and crushing it.*

" 'The ten horns are ten kings who will come from this kingdom. *After them another king will arise, different from the earlier ones; he will subdue three kings.*

" *'He will speak against the Most High and oppress his saints and try to change the set times and the laws. The saints will be handed over to him for a time, times and half a time.*

" 'But the court will sit, and his power will be taken away and completely destroyed forever.

" 'Then the sovereignty, power and greatness of the kingdoms under the whole heaven will be handed over to the saints, the people of the Most High. His kingdom will be an everlasting kingdom, and all rulers will worship and obey him.'

"This is the end of the matter. I, Daniel, was deeply troubled by my thoughts, and my face turned pale, but I kept the matter to myself."

Daniel is viewing the sequence of beastly influences, and they rule a series of kingdoms on earth. Under the beasts are kings who rule the daily affairs of the kingdom, but supporting these kings are the beastly forces. The fourth beast is different from all the previous beasts, and the fourth kingdom is different from all the previous kingdoms. After the reign of ten kings, under the influence of the fourth beast, an eleventh king shall rise to power, different from all the others:

Dan. 7:25   He [the eleventh king] will speak

against the Most High and oppress his saints
and try to change the set times and the laws.
The saints will be handed over to him for a
time, times and half a time.

The fourth beast makes war against the saints and
prevails! However, it is only until the Ancient of Days
comes. Then, the Ancient of Days judges the world and
finds in favor of the saints of the Most High. Conse-
quently, the saints inherit the kingdoms of the earth.

In the final chapter of the Book of Daniel, the prophet
sees another great vision of the End Times.

The angel says that during this period of struggle between the holy people and the earthly ruler, many will
succeed in "purifying themselves and making themselves white and refined, but the wicked will grow in
wickedness; none of the wicked will understand, but
those who are wise will understand." (Dan. 12:10) The
power of the holy people in the earth will be zero, wickedness will reign; then, the Ancient of Days will move
with the help of the archangel Michael and judge the
earth, ultimately giving it over to the holy people.

In the Book of the Revelation, this pattern is repeated
but with different symbols. A pure woman, "wrapped in
the sun and standing on the moon" is pregnant with the
Messianic ruler of the earth. She delivers the child who
will rule the earth with an iron hand. The archangel
Michael drives the dragon out of heaven.

Rev. 12:14   The woman was given the two
wings of a great eagle, so that she might fly to
the place prepared for her in the desert, where
she would be taken care of for a time, times
and halftimes, out of the serpent's reach.

The dragon is so furious about this that he makes war

with all her other offspring for generations. At this point in the Revelation, we see the rising up of the beast who will rule the earth and war against the children of God, just as we saw in Daniel. However, at the end of the stated time, times and halftimes, the Holy One moves in and makes judgment upon the earth, separating the wicked from the seekers of God. And the seekers inherit the earth.

THE MICROCOSM AND MACROCOSM OF INTERPRETATION

Material that comes from the deeper consciousness of an individual can have two dimensions to it: microcosmic and macrocosmic. In other words, it reflects conditions *within* and *without*, or above and below, in heaven and in earth, in flesh and in spirit, in an individual and in the universe. This concept was first taught by Hermes in ancient Egypt. His teaching was stated: "As within so without, as above so below." It has been extensively elaborated upon in the Edgar Cayce readings, interpreting much of the Revelation with a *micro*cosmic understanding of this strange collection of images.[1] Carl Jung's ideas and examples have also added much to our understanding of how and why this occurs.[2]

If one doesn't acknowledge the duality of micro- and macrocosms (universes), one tends to only look outside of oneself for the interpretation. But much of what is being seen deals with the inner person, too.

Despite being in the dimension of phantoms and inner imagery, there is a humanlike person who comes to help Daniel with the interpretation. Daniel describes him as "one like a son of man." He tells Daniel that the four beasts in his dream are four kingdoms that will rise from the earth. But the saints of the Most High will ultimately "receive the kingdom and will possess it forever—

yes, for ever and ever." Now, most of us would immediately take this to mean the outer world of nations, governments and peoples. But, it also relates to the inner world of organs, glands and cells—attitudes, emotions and thoughts. When one is in the spirit and the inner mind, the term "the earth" can mean the body as well as the world. When the humanlike person says, "the saints of the Most High," he can be speaking of those cells and organs within a body that have been rejuvenated with the spirit of health and Life.

With this in mind, let's examine some of the elements of Daniel's vision—remembering that we are actually angelic, spiritual beings inside human, fleshly bodies.

"The four beasts" is an archetypal imagery found throughout the Bible. Here are two more examples:

> Ezek. 1:10   Each of the four had the face of a man, and on the right side each had the face of a lion, and on the left the face of an ox; each also had the face of an eagle.

> Rev. 4:7   The first living creature was like a lion, the second was like an ox, the third had a face like a man, the fourth was like a flying eagle.

Notice the similarity in these beasts. In fact, both Ezekiel and John, though their visions are hundreds of years apart, see a man, lion, ox, and eagle. Daniel sees a lion, bear, leopard, and a terrible beast. Perhaps Daniel's fourth beast was like a man, but so viciously horrifying he could not call it such.

These beasts represent four lower, earthly forces *within* the human body, as well as four earthly powers in the outer world. Psalm 57:4 beautifully expresses our plight with these inner and outer forces: "I am in the midst of lions; I lie among ravenous beasts—men whose teeth are spears and arrows, whose tongues are sharp swords." Daniel's fourth beast has teeth that crush its victims. Perhaps the psalmist and Daniel were seeing the same beastly aspect of humanity—powerfully destructive forces within and around us.

St. John eventually sees another beast that incorporates all of Daniel's beasts into one: Rev. 13:2 "The beast I saw resembled a leopard, but had feet like those of a bear and a mouth like that of a lion. The dragon gave the beast his power and his throne and great authority." This last sentence alludes to the ancient teaching that within each of us is a vital life-force (kundalini), which is often symbolized as a serpent or dragon that moves through power centers within our bodies (chakras). Therefore, John's comment that "the dragon gives the beast his power," fits well with these teachings. In fact, "chakras" is a Sanskrit word that means "wheels," and flaming wheels appear in Ezekiel's and Daniel's visions.

> Dan. 7:9   As I looked, thrones were set in place, and the Ancient of Days took his seat. His clothing was as white as snow; the hair of his head was white like wool. His throne was flaming with fire, and *its wheels were all ablaze.*
>
> Ezek. 1:15   As I looked at the living creatures, I saw a wheel on the ground beside each creature with its four faces.
> Ezek. 1:20   Wherever the spirit would go, they would go, and the wheels would rise along with them, *because the spirit of the living creatures was in the wheels.*
> Ezek. 10:13   I heard the wheels being called *"the whirling wheels."*

"Whirling wheels" is almost exactly how the ancients described the spiritual chakras in the human body. Each chakra is associated with attitudes, emotions, and urges within every human. The Cayce readings say that the endocrine glands are at the core of the chakra forces (pituitary, pineal, thyroid, thymus, adrenals, cells of Leydig, gonads—seven total). Cayce also says that when St. John sees the seven candles, the seven flames, the seven stars, and the seven churches, he is seeing these spiritual centers within himself. When these forces begin to catch fire with the movement of the life force, or élan vital, or kundalini energy, then they begin to whirl, and our godly selves begin to gain power again—for weal or woe.

The body is the ultimate temple of the Living God. John 2:21: "The temple he [Jesus] had spoken of was his body." 2 Cor. 6:16: "We are the temple of the living God." All the imagery of the prophets includes visions into these inner processes. Out of the fleshly part of us will come the heavenly one. The battles, purgings and, ultimately, the Messiah will first come *within* each of us. Of course, it will all come in the outer world, as well.

THE GREAT AND TERRIBLE DAY
OF THE COMING OF THE LORD

Because the coming of the higher self, or the godly self, is so profoundly overwhelming to the earthly self, it is often seen as a disaster for the lower self, or the human self. In a manner of speaking, it is the death of the lower self and the birth of the divine self. As the life force of the spirit begins to stir—or, as Daniel put it, "the four winds of heaven churning up the great sea" (7:2)—the spiritual centers within the body begin to whirl, and the great powers are aroused. They are at first like beasts. "I was like a beast before Thee." (Psalm 73:22) But once subdued, they serve the Lord of the house.

In the Cayce material, the first four chakras are where most of our consciousness and energy exist. If we never control our urges nor aspire to anything greater than gratification, then they become the four beasts that we are so familiar with: sex, possessiveness, violence, and selfishness — the very stuff that every TV ad man knows will sell product. On the other hand, if we do control ourselves and aspire to more, then the life force creates higher energies in these centers, and it moves upward into the top three chakras. There it will be tested again, either to be found beastly or heavenly—and another battle ensues until the higher self is victorious.

It is a dangerous awakening. One can become a beast or an angel, depending upon what the dominant influence is. If it is self and gratification or glorification of self, then the beastly nature takes hold. If it is an attunement with the Creator and its ways, then the angelic one takes hold. And since others are in various stages of development with these energies, people can become beastly or angelic in their interaction with one another. The spirit of cooperation, mutual respect and a sense of the oneness of humanity, or the brother- sisterhood, are needed to help all of us rise to higher levels.

Here's how the prophets have seen "the great and terrible day of the coming of the Lord." However, let's consider that the name *Lord* in this context is also referring to the overself, the godly self, that part that was created in the image of the Creator. From Isaiah to Peter we have remarkably similar and consistent imagery:

> Isa. 13:6   Wail, for the day of the Lord is near; it will come like destruction from the Almighty.
> Isa. 13:9   See, the day of the Lord is coming—a cruel day, with wrath and fierce anger—to make the land desolate and destroy the sinners within it.

Ezek. 30:3   For the day is near, the day of the
Lord is near—a day of clouds, a time of doom
for the nations.

Joel 1:15   Alas for that day! For the day of the
Lord is near; it will come like destruction from
the Almighty.

Joel 2:1-2   Let all who live in the land tremble,
for the day of the Lord is coming. It is close at
hand—a day of darkness and gloom, a day of
clouds and blackness. Like dawn spreading
across the mountains a large and mighty army
comes, such as never was of old nor ever will
be in ages to come.

Joel 2:11   The Lord thunders at the head of
his army; his forces are beyond number, and
mighty are those who obey his command. The
day of the Lord is great; it is dreadful. Who can
endure it?

Joel 2:31   The sun will be turned to darkness and the moon to blood before the coming
of the great and dreadful day of the Lord.

Joel 3:14 Multitudes, multitudes in the valley of *decision!* For the day of the Lord is near
in the valley of *decision.*

Amos 5:18-20   Woe to you who long for the
day of the Lord! Why do you long for the day of
the Lord? That day will be darkness, not light.
It will be as though a man fled from a lion only
to meet a bear, as though he entered his house
and rested his hand on the wall only to have a
snake bite him. Will not the day of the Lord be
darkness, not light—pitch-dark, without a ray
of brightness?

Obad. 15   The day of the Lord is near for all nations. As you have done, it will be done to you; your deeds will return upon your own head.

Zeph. 1:7   Be silent before the Sovereign Lord, for the day of the Lord is near. The Lord has prepared a sacrifice; he has consecrated those he has invited.
Zeph. 1:14   The great day of the Lord is near—near and coming quickly. Listen! The cry on the day of the Lord will be bitter, the shouting of the warrior there.

Zech. 14:1   A day of the Lord is coming when your plunder will be divided among you.

Mal. 4:5   See, I will send you the prophet Elijah before that great and dreadful day of the Lord comes.

Acts 2:20   The sun will be turned to darkness and the moon to blood before the coming of the great and glorious day of the Lord.

1 Cor. 5:5   Hand this man over to Satan, so that the sinful nature may be destroyed and his spirit saved on the day of the Lord.

1 Ths. 5:2   You know very well that the day of the Lord will come like a thief in the night.

2 Pet. 3:10   But the day of the Lord will come like a thief. The heavens will disappear with a roar; the elements will be destroyed by fire, and the earth and everything in it will be laid bare.

All of these statements have been quoted over and over to set the fear of God into people. But what these prophets were seeing was the human-self's reaction to the end of its dominance, the end times, and the beginning of the divine-self's reign, forever and ever.

St. Paul's statement above is surprising (1Cor. 5:5). He actually calls for one to be handed over to Satan for purging before the coming of the Lord. But if you recall, this is exactly the mission God gave Satan in the book of Job.

> Job 1:8-12   Then the Lord said to Satan, "Have you considered my servant Job? There is no one on earth like him; he is blameless and upright, a man who fears God and shuns evil."
>
> "Does Job fear God for nothing?" Satan replied. "Have you not put a hedge around him and his household and everything he has? You have blessed the work of his hands, so that his flocks and herds are spread throughout the land. But stretch out your hand and strike everything he has, and he will surely curse you to your face."
>
> The Lord said to Satan, "Very well, then, everything he has is in your hands, but on the man himself do not lay a finger." Then Satan went out from the presence of the Lord.

In the ancient Hebrew teachings, Satan (literally, "adversary") is the accuser, as we see when he first speaks to God in Job, accusing Job of loving God only as long as his earthly self is satisfied. But, he also becomes God's tester, putting Job to the test of his faith and patience.

Notice also how Satan first asks God to test Job's outer world, his possessions. When Job passes this test, then Satan seeks to test the inner world of Job's own being.

The macro- and microcosms are important for us to understand.

Finally, in the New Testament, Satan becomes the tempter. As the Holy Spirit comes upon us (as it did Jesus), we will be led out into the desert to be tested, tempted, and prepared for the coming of the Lord within our beings and outside among others and the world—until, like Jesus, we can say, "Be gone Satan, you have no part in me."[3]

THE SPIRITUALIZED "SON OF MAN" OR "MESSIAH" COMES

Daniel and the other prophets see the power of the heavens come upon these lower forces to judge and subdue or destroy them. Heaven in this context symbolizes our higher, godly selves coming more into control of our being, and subduing these beastly forces. While in the macrocosm, the great Spirit, God and Its forces, come and subdue these influences throughout the world.

Here are descriptions of the coming of the spirit:

> Ezek. 1:25—2:2   Then there came a voice from above the expanse over their heads [the beasts' heads] as they stood with lowered wings. [The beasts are in a submissive pose, and the higher self is descending from the higher chakras to take command of the entire body-temple.]
>
> Above the expanse over their heads was what looked like a throne of sapphire, and high above on the throne was a figure like that of a man. [But this is the being with whom God originally shared the Garden.]
>
> I saw that from what appeared to be his waist up he looked like glowing metal, as if full

of fire, and that from there down he looked like fire; and brilliant light surrounded him.

Like the appearance of a rainbow in the clouds on a rainy day, so was the radiance around him. This was the appearance of the likeness of the glory of the Lord. When I saw it, I fell face-down, and I heard the voice of one speaking.

He said to me, "Son of man, stand up on your feet and I will speak to you."

As he spoke, *the Spirit came into me* and raised me to my feet, and I heard him speaking to me.

Rev. 1:12-18   I turned around to see the voice that was speaking to me. And when I turned I saw seven golden lampstands, and among the lampstands was someone "like a son of man," dressed in a robe reaching down to his feet and with a golden sash around his chest.

His head and hair were white like wool, as white as snow, and his eyes were like blazing fire.

His feet were like bronze glowing in a furnace, and his voice was like the sound of rushing waters.

In his right hand he held seven stars, and out of his mouth came a sharp double-edged sword. His face was like the sun shining in all its brilliance.

When I saw him, I fell at his feet as though dead. Then he placed his right hand on me and said: "Do not be afraid. *I am the First and the Last. I am the Living One; I was dead, and behold I am alive for ever and ever!* And I hold the keys of death and Hades." [This is the portion of us that died when we left the spiritual attunement for the earthly, physical life. Therefore, it was alive, was dead and behold is alive again.]

Rev. 10:1   Then I saw another mighty angel coming down from heaven. He was robed in a cloud, with a rainbow above his head: his face was like the sun, and his legs were like fiery pillars.

Rev. 14:14   I looked, and there before me was a white cloud, and seated on the cloud was one "like a son of man" with a crown of gold on his head and a sharp sickle in his hand.

Each of these great visionaries saw the beastly urges of humanity make war with the heavenly forces of God and the godlings, but the heavenly forces ultimately win and rule forever. This is occurring within each person. We each call forth our better selves, wrestle with our worst selves and, with the help of God, we are ultimately victorious, becoming greater than even the angels for having been put to the test, the struggle and been found worthy.[4] As St. John says, "I, John, [am] your brother and companion in the suffering and kingdom and patient endurance that are ours in Jesus . . . " (Rev. 1:9)

Of course, our primary interest in this book is the prophecies of the End Times in the outer world. However, it is important to keep in mind Hermes' great teaching, because the inner and outer cannot be totally isolated. Ultimately, they are one. But for our purposes here, we'll look at them separately.

CYCLES, RHYTHMS, AND SOUL GROUPS

In order to fully understand how an ancient dream can have any bearing on our present time, we must understand the rhythms of Life. Everything occurs in rhythms or cycles. When the mystery schools use the circle as the highest symbol of wisdom, it is because it is an emblem of the way life is. The ancient symbols of the circular serpent with its tail in its mouth and the goddess whose toes touch the top of her head to form a circle with her body are emblems of the circumferential movement or rhythm of life, in which the beginning is ultimately the ending.

Therefore, when the "son of man" in Daniel's dream interprets the horns as kingdoms, and then identifies the kingdoms as the Medes, the Persians, and the Greeks, he is not simply speaking of their activities during Daniel's time, but a recurring cycle of these soul groups and their interaction with one another throughout the history of this realm. Their influence will return again and again, with different names, perhaps, but similar circumstances, until the End Time comes. It is the way of things in this world—history repeats itself. Life pulsates. We move from activity to inactivity to activity again, from life to death to life again, from imagery to darkness to imagery again, from awake to sleep to awake again. Therefore, when the angel Gabriel says that Daniel's vision is a vision that "concerns the time of the end" and "the distant future," he is telling the truth.

To develop this idea of recurring cycles a little further, let's consider Daniel's dream of the outer world as we would an inner-world dream. Then, Media, Persia, and Greece could be understood as symbols of different attitudes, urges, and perspectives in life. In both his first and second vision, Daniel is told that the horns represent these three kingdoms and their wrestling with one another for power and influence. In one of Cayce's readings about the coming of the Messiah, he actually makes a reference to the ancient Persian king, Xerxes! Why? What could ancient Xerxes have to do with the coming of the Messiah?

Xerxes was a powerful ruler of Persia who wanted to conquer the Greeks. Xerxes raised the largest army in history (at that time). But the way Xerxes got to Greece was through the aid of *the second church of John's Revelation*, Ephesus! Here's where Cayce's reference comes into play in our times. Cayce states it this way: " . . . when there is the turning back from the raising up of Xerxes as the deliverer from an unknown tongue or land, *and again is there seen that this occurs* in the entrance of the Messiah in this period—1998." (5748-5) Clearly, Cayce is seeing the cycle coming around again; a cycle that began in ancient times. According to his view, the spiritual seekers looked to Xerxes (an earthly power) to deliver them from Greece's power and, in so doing, let his power take hold of them. It is trading one earthly master for another. Judas Iscariot looked to the man Jesus to deliver his people from the Romans with violence and power, but the man Jesus was looking to the Spirit to deliver them all from the powers of the flesh and the world. As Jesus said to Peter when Peter wanted him to avoid his prophesied destiny, "Get behind me, Satan! You are a stumbling block to me; you do not have in mind the things of God, but the things of men." (Matt. 16:23)

When we turn away from seeking our deliverer in the flesh and seek him through our attunement to the Spirit, then we see the Messiah's true influence. For our true liberation comes from the Spirit, not the flesh. Remember, in Daniel's visions, the great beastly ruler was not overthrown "by human power."

Who or what influence and power is represented by Xerxes today? In what way is humanity still looking for its deliverance through earthly forces? Perhaps it is what the great Russian writer, Leo Tolstoy, foresaw on his deathbed — a vision of a great anti-christ coming in the future. It was a gigantic angel of darkness covering the whole earth, and across its chest was a banner that read,

"Commercialism." We have seen four great powers attempt to take hold of the world in the 1900's: capitalism, fascism, communism, and socialism. But none of these has been as powerfully captivating as the great force of *commercialism*. Every country has been affected by this force and its master, *materialism*. Now, most humans on earth are bombarded with hypnotic persuasions to buy-buy, possess-possess, consume-consume. Once sacred events are now brought to us by the grace and power of corporations whose primary goal is to sell product—for example, "the Olympics, brought to you by Coca-Cola and NBC." Tolstoy was shaken by what he saw, but he couldn't possibly have seen just how awesome this force would become across the world. The earth is covered with ads. All the great holy days are now commercialized holidays. The sacred images are replaced with the profane (e.g., Easter bunny, Santa Claus). The birthday of the Father of our country, George Washington, is now listed among the greatest shopping days. The ideals for which he struggled are lost in a buying spree.

Perhaps materialism, combined with commercialism, fits Daniel's vision that: "The fourth beast is a fourth kingdom that will appear on earth. It will be different from all the other kingdoms *and will devour the whole earth*, trampling it down and crushing it." No country or economic system is immune to the desires and lusts of its people. Eventually, these forces will overwhelm the country. Seeing the material wealth of the Western world and Japan, much of the rest of the world has lusted for their part in this. But they don't often see the dark side of materialism. Material wealth comes with a price. Usually, that price is the suppression, or at least the limitation, of our spiritual nature and the accentuating of our lower nature.

Now, one's attempts to awaken to the Spirit, to seek the spirit's desires, to give birth to one's spiritual nature, and attune to God, are constantly challenged by the forces that demand material consumption, possession, and gratification. Mammon is what it sells, and in order to keep selling it, it must possess the consciousness of individuals, filling them with unending desire for more, more, more. But as the Master said, "No one can serve two masters. Either he will hate the one and love the other, or he will be devoted to the one and despise the other. You cannot serve both God and mammon." (Matt. 6:24)

True seekers of the spirit are constantly in a struggle with mammon's pull on them. In Psalm 73 the great seeker Asaph writes about his own struggle against envying the power of material possessions in this world. He almost lost his footing on the spiritual path because of it: "But I almost stumbled, my feet came close to slipping. For I was envious of the arrogant. I saw their prosperity. They have increased in wealth. Surely in vain I have kept my heart pure, and washed my hands in innocence. When I pondered to understand this, it was troublesome in my sight; until I came into the sanctuary of God; then I perceived their end. As for me, the nearness of God is my good." (Excerpts from Psalm 73)

The greatest beast to challenge the holy people may well be materialism and its companion, commercialism. It breeds and supports desires for outer-world things. It causes the children of God to spend their resources of time, space, and consciousness in the pursuit of more material gratification. On the Mt. of Olives, Jesus warns that in the latter days, powerful deceivers will come to lead us off into outer pursuits, even *outer* pursuits of God. Yet, the kingdom of God is *within* us. It is spirit not matter. It is life, not food. It is the beauty of a loving heart and a smiling face, not clothing and image. But the commercial forces would have us believe that "image is everything;" material life is "where it's at." They create a reality in which contentment is found in consumption and possessions. Coke is "the real thing." They even take sacred sayings and turn them around for the profane—instead of "Jesus saves," we have "Datsun saves."

Jesus spent much of his time fighting these ideas:

> Matt. 6:26   Consider the birds of the air; they do not sow or reap or store away in barns, and yet your heavenly Father feeds them. Are you not much more valuable than they?
>
> Matt. 6:28-30   And why do you worry about clothes? See how the lilies of the field grow. They do not labor or spin. Yet I tell you, not even Solomon in all his splendor was dressed like one of these. If that is how God clothes the grass of the field, which is here today and tomorrow is thrown into the fire, will he not much more clothe you, O you of little faith?
>
> Matt. 19:21   Jesus answered, "If you want to be perfect, go, sell your possessions and give to the poor, and you will have treasure in heaven. Then come, follow me."

> Luke 12:33   Sell your possessions and give to the poor. Provide purses for yourselves that will not wear out, a treasure in heaven that will not be exhausted, where no thief comes near and no moth destroys.

In The Revelation, St. John sees the ultimate beast, and everyone who serves it must wear its mark upon them: "No one could buy or sell unless he had the mark, which is the name of the beast or the number of his name." (13:17) Tolstoy may have seen the greatest beast to challenge the children of God from realizing their true potential.

For a balanced perspective on this issue, we need to

also note that Jesus expressed a sense of decency and order in the material world by his teaching that we should "render unto Caesar that which is Caesar's and unto God that which is God's."[5] He, too, paid his taxes when the tax collector came[6]—revealing again his sense of cooperation and balance. What I believe he was teaching in the previously quoted passages is to "render unto God that which is God's." We tend to forget this part when we get into money, things, and other earthly desires.

DANIEL'S SECOND VISION

Daniel's second vision is like the first, even though it occurred two years later. It contains three important changes that will indicate the end time is at hand: (1) the daily sacrifice was ended, (2) no one was entering the sanctuary, and (3) the holy people were being trampled. This all leads to the "abomination of desolation" that Daniel sees and Jesus refers to in his talk on the Mt. of Olives.

1) The Daily Sacrifice

The daily sacrifice refers to the offering up of outer-self's interests for inner-self's nourishment. This is done by setting aside time, space, and consciousness for the spirit rather than the flesh. Few are doing this. It also refers to the sacrifice of self for another—getting out of one's self-centered world and caring about others. Jesus taught that no love is greater than that which sets asides one's interests for anothers'.[7] The Cayce readings say that Jesus' private prayer was, "Others, Lord, others." Rather than being consumed with our needs, we need to shift our consciousness and think of others' needs. This causes us to move out of individualness and more into universalness; to move from the little picture to the big picture. It expands us. I personally have found that when life is at its most dissatisfying, the best thing to do is look for someone who needs some help, and help them. It gets your mind off your problems and, before you know it, you feel better, and your perspective seems clearer than before. It doesn't have to be something grand. Just helping someone move, fix something, or make a connection, etc., can suffice. There's a magic in this that creates health—mental, emotional, and physical health. Unfortunately, our culture attempts to solve dissatisfaction with food, appearance, medicine, or even more focus on self! We need to remember the benefits of sacrifice, both for inner nourishment and physical health.

2) The Entering of the Sanctuary

The entering of the sanctuary refers to the movement of consciousness into the inner recesses of our being, where the spirit and kingdom of God abide. This is done through deep prayer, inner reflection, inner listening, and meditation. There are examples of Jesus' practice of seeking time, space, and consciousness so that he could enter the inner sanctuary:

> Matt. 14:23   After he had dismissed them, he went up on a mountainside by himself to pray. When evening came, he was there alone.

> Luke 6:12   One of those days Jesus went out to a mountainside to pray, and spent the night praying to God.

> Matt. 26:36   Then Jesus went with his disciples to a place called Gethsemane, and he said to them, "Sit here while I go over there and pray."

> Mark 1:35   Very early in the morning, while it
> was still dark, Jesus got up, left the house and
> went off to a solitary place, where he prayed.

The modern world doesn't set aside time, space, and
consciousness for attunement to the Spirit. Religious
services have become social engagements, outer greeting and talking events, not inner attunements. The sanctuary is within us. In order to get there, one has to go off
to a quiet place and be still. As the psalm says: "Be still
and know that I am God." (Psalm 46:10)[8] The Holy of Holies is left empty and unattended—both in the inner
world of one's own microcosm and in the outer world of
the macrocosm.

The Cayce readings say, "Mind and soul are the taber-
nacle." (1479-1) And in reading 2067-1, Cayce identifies
the outer court of the temple as the body, the inner court
as the mind, and the Holy of Holies as the spirit. Each
person is the temple of the living God, laid out just as the
outer temple.

Ezekiel receives this message in his vision when the
Lord says, "Because you have defiled my sanctuary with
all your vile images and detestable practices, I myself will
withdraw . . . " (Ezek. 5:11) This certainly sounds like the
Lord is speaking of our inner sanctuary, where images
abound.

3) The Trampling of the Holy People

The trampling of the holy people refers to the constant
suppression of the influence of the God-seekers by the
forces that control the world. Spiritual pursuits are often
suppressed by the forces of materialism, unless of course
there's a commercial opportunity involved! Even religious television shows spend much of their time solicit-
ing their viewers for more mammon, which in turn
causes their viewers to go seek more mammnon—and

on and on it goes. "Trampling of the holy people" is also considered to be a reference to the attempted extermination of the Jews by the Nazis; an act that ultimately drove the Jews (whom Daniel would have considered to be "the holy people") to return to their homeland, restore their nation, and become self-reliant again. All of which is foreshadowed in the prophecies of the end times!

DANIEL'S THIRD VISION

Dan. 9:20-24   While I was speaking and praying, confessing my sin and the sin of my people Israel and making my request to the Lord my God for his holy hill—while I was still in prayer, *Gabriel,* the man I had seen in the earlier vision, came to me in swift flight about the time of the evening sacrifice.

He instructed me and said to me, *"Daniel, I have now come to give you insight and understanding.*

"As soon as you began to pray, an answer was given, which I have come to tell you, for you are highly esteemed. Therefore, consider the message and understand the vision:

"Seventy 'sevens' are decreed for your people and your holy city to finish transgression, to put an end to sin, to atone for wickedness, to bring in everlasting righteousness, to seal up vision and prophecy and to anoint the most holy."

Well, here is the whole plan, clearly stated: The seekers ("your people") must: (1) finish with their self-seeking, (2) atone for their mistakes, (3) bring everlasting righteousness into their lives and the lives of those around them, and (4) anoint the Messiah—the messiah *within* each of us and the Messiah *without* for the world.

A set amount of time has been decreed for this to happen: seventy cycles of sevens.

It continues:

> "Know and understand this: *From the issuing of the decree to restore and rebuild Jerusalem until the Messiah, the ruler, comes, there will be seven 'sevens,' and sixty-two 'sevens.'* It will be rebuilt with streets and a trench, but in times of trouble.
>
> *"After the sixty-two 'sevens,' the Messiah will be cut off and will have nothing.* The people of the ruler who will come will destroy the city and the sanctuary. The end will come like a flood: War will continue until the end, and desolations have been decreed.
>
> "He [the earthly ruler who will come] will confirm a covenant with many for one 'seven.' In the middle of the 'seven' he will put an end to sacrifice and offering. And on a wing [of the temple] he will set up *an abomination that causes desolation*, until the end that is decreed is poured out on him." (25-27)

Since the rebuilding of the temple and the coming of the Messiah is a recurring theme, we need to understand this better. In attempting to understand the phrase: "From the issuing of the decree to restore and rebuild Jerusalem until the Messiah comes, there will be seven sevens;" we need a little history lesson.

The temple in Jerusalem was first built by Solomon "in the four hundred and eightieth year after the people of Israel came out of the land of Egypt, in the fourth year of Solomon's reign over Israel, in the month of Ziv." This would be April-May of approximately 1440 B.C., though most scholars prefer 960 B.C.[9] This great temple was destroyed in 587-6 B.C. by the Babylonians.[10] It was rebuilt in the second year of Darius I, 520 B.C.,[11] and destroyed again by Titus in 70 A.D. It has not been rebuilt. Upon its site is now the Islamic mosque, Dome of the Rock.

Daniel's visions occurred in the years 554, 552, and 535 B.C. Clearly, the temple and Jerusalem were rebuilt *after* Daniel's visions, in 520 B.C. and then destroyed again in 70 A.D. There appears to be a cycle here. Built in 960, destroyed in 586, rebuilt in 520, destroyed in 70. Since Gabriel said that the vision was of the distant future and the times of the end, we can assume the temple will be rebuilt again.

The Edgar Cayce readings teach that the vision of Daniel, especially chapter 12, refers to WWII. Cayce also said that one of the purposes of WWII was to begin the return of the Jews to Israel in 1947. Then, we can assume that the phrase, "from the decree to rebuild and restore Jerusalem, until the Messiah comes, there will be seven sevens," might well be speaking of this period. If 1947 is the year of the decree to restore Israel's Jerusalem, then adding 49 years (i.e., "seven sevens") onto 1947 would mean that 1996 is the year of the coming of the Messiah. The Cayce readings say, 1998. Nostradamus implies 1999. The Holy Mother seems to be indicating that it coincides with the end of the line of Popes, which she says ends with this current Pope. So, I think we can say that there is prophetic agreement that the coming of the Messiah may occur somewhere between 1996 and 1999. Of course, many have tried to figure this out before us, and have come up with different ideas, but there is supporting evidence for this time frame: 1996 to 1999.

If we consider what this means within ourselves, then from the time that we issue the decree to rebuild our holy consciousness and the temples of our bodies for the abiding of our godly selves, it will take seven seven-year cycles until the messiah comes within us. This idea fits

very well with Cayce's teachings that the body completely rebuilds itself every seven years and that we will
indeed have new bodies during the period when the
Messiah reigns for a thousand years of peace. Cayce references St. Paul's comments on this:

> 1 Cor. 15:51-52   Listen, I tell you a mystery: We
> will not all sleep, but we will all be changed—
> in a flash, in the twinkling of an eye, at the last
> trumpet. For the trumpet will sound, the dead
> will be raised imperishable, and we will be
> changed.

In Cayce's comments about a "new root race," he explains that the human race is on the verge of another
major change in its body structure. He says that what St.
Paul is referring to is just that, a new body. The body
structure that we currently inhabit is approximately
40,000 years old. In other words, scientists can find remains dating as far back as 40,000 years ago that match
our present bodies. Beyond that time period, all human-
oid remains are different from our present structure. Is it
a coincidence that 40 is once again the unit involved
here?—Noah's 40 days and nights, Israel's 40 years in the
desert, Moses' staying on the mountain with God for 40
days and nights, Jesus' 40 days and nights, etc, and our
bodies being 40,000 years old. Perhaps a change is about
to happen, because the cycle has come around to the
appropriate moment.

Now what then is meant by the phrase, "After the sixty-
two (sevens) the Messiah will be cut off and will have
nothing"? (Dan. 9:26) Then it goes on to say that the
people and the ruler who is to come will put an end to
the city and sanctuary (i.e., Jerusalem and the temple),
and will put an end to sacrifice and offering, and will set
up an abomination that causes desolation. This will hap-

pen until the end time comes upon this ruler and his people. What does this mean?

The Christian answer is that the Israelites' John the Baptist and Jesus of Nazareth were the prophecied return of Elijah and the Messiah, respectively, and that the Messiah reigned for a time and then was cut off. His temple (body) was destroyed, but resurrected, and ultimately the outer temple was destroyed (70 A.D.). The Israelites were then scattered throughout the earth, until the time of the end drew near—when they would be called back to restore and rebuild Jerusalem and the temple. In the meantime, "the people and their ruler" were the Gentiles and the spirit of materialism and earthly power that has reigned for these past two thousand years. But the age of the Gentiles is coming to an end, and the Messiah will return with power, and all will be changed.

THE ARMAGEDDON

The only biblical passage to use this name is in the Book of Revelation. Here are the relevant verses:

> Rev. 16:13-19   Then I saw three evil spirits that looked like frogs; they came out of the mouth of the dragon, out of the mouth of the beast and out of the mouth of the false prophet. They are spirits of demons performing miraculous signs, and they go out to the kings of the whole world, to gather them for the battle on the great day of God Almighty. "Behold, I come like a thief! Blessed is he who stays awake and keeps his clothes with him, so that he may not go naked and be shamefully exposed." Then they gathered the kings together to the

place that in Hebrew is called *Armageddon.* The seventh angel poured out his bowl into the air, and out of the temple came a loud voice from the throne, saying, "It is done!" Then there came flashes of lightning, rumblings, peals of thunder and a severe earthquake. No earthquake like it has ever occurred since man has been on earth, so tremendous was the quake. The great city split into three parts, and the cities of the nations collapsed. God remembered Babylon the Great and gave her the cup filled with the wine of the fury of his wrath.

Notice how this event is marked by a severe earth change, an earthquake like none other man has seen on earth! Armageddon literally means, "Hill of Megiddo," the site of several decisive battles in Israel's history (see Jg. 5:19, 2 Kg. 9:27 and 2 Chr. 35:22). The reference to "The great city" is believed by many to be Rome, a city the disciple John would have considered to be a great earthly power at his time. Babylon the Great would be symbolic of materiality and commercialism at its most contrary to spirituality and community. Changes in Rome are also seen by Nostradamus and Mother Mary as a key sign of the coming of the End Times.

At this point, let's read what Jesus says on the Mt. of Olives.

JESUS' TEACHING ON THE MOUNT OF OLIVES

Matt. 24:1-3 Jesus left the temple and was walking away when his disciples came up to him to call his attention to its buildings. [This would have been about 33 A.D.]

"Do you see all these things?" he asked. "I tell you the truth, not one stone here will be

left on another; every one will be thrown
down." [The temple was destroyed in 70 A.D.]

As Jesus was sitting on the Mount of Olives,
the disciples came to him privately. "Tell us,"
they said, *"when will this happen, and what
will be the sign of your coming and of the end of
the age?"*

Our earthly selves naturally tend to understand time
and prophecy from a *linear* perspective—first this will
happen, then this and finally that. However, our higher
selves and the spiritual realm see time and prophecy
from a holistic perspective—this has, is, and will happen
again and again until the rhythm, the pulse, the cycle is
complete. Therefore, a great visionary can be speaking
of a distant future as well as an imminent present. So,
when Jesus answers what appears to us to be a question
about the immediate future, he may actually be giving
a more holistic answer. And later, when he says—"I
tell you the truth, this generation will certainly not
pass away until all these things have happened."—he
may be correct, even though all these disciples died
before the end times. Those listening to him will experience every bit of it within their microcosms, and ultimately within the macrocosm. Remember, all the dead
will be called to life again.[12] The Mt. Olives' teaching continues:

Matt. 24:4-8   Jesus answered: "Watch out that
no one deceives you.

"For many will come in my name, claiming,
'I am the Messiah,'[13] and will deceive many.

"You will hear of wars and rumors of wars,
but see to it that you are not alarmed. Such
things must happen, but the end is still to
come.

"Nation will rise against nation, and kingdom against kingdom. There will be famines
and earthquakes in various places.
All these are the beginning of birth pains."

See how Jesus uses this metaphor to explain the suffering and changes that must come about. The End
Times are the birth of the Spirit. Like a woman in labor,
we will suffer pain in our attempts to deliver our spiritual selves. The teaching continues:

Matt. 24:9-11   "Then you will be handed over
to be persecuted and put to death, and you will
be hated by all nations because of me.
    "At that time *many will turn away from the
faith* and will betray and hate each other, and
*many false prophets will appear and deceive
many people."*

In the 1900s we have seen the falling away from the
faith. Who can forget the New York Times' headline: "God
is dead!" And the false prophets have become so common that many deceived seekers have already been
deprogrammed! But they keep coming. Some in the
guise of religious leaders, some as political leaders, some
as psychological liberators. Another amazing phenomenon has been the paganizing of the country that was
founded with the slogan, "In God We Trust," printed on
its money. The freedom this country provided the world
has been used against it to undermine its values and
purposes. Now, instead of a healthy separation of
Church and State, we have a State that can have no sem-
blance of trusting in or calling upon God.
    The Mt. Olives' teaching continues:

Matt. 9:12-13   "Because of the increase of

lawlessness, the love of most will grow cold, but
he who stands firm to the end will be saved."

If there is one prophecy that I feel we all can point to
for evidence that we are in the latter days, it is this one.
From Asia, through the U.S. and Europe and on into Russia, the Middle East, and India, lawlessness has taken a
hold on daily life that has not been seen before. Crime is
everywhere. Some countries are actually ruled by crime
forces. Many fear the newly dissolved Soviet Union has
left Russia a lawless country run by the forces of the un-
derworld.

The Mt. Olives' teaching continues:

> Matt. 9:14   "And this gospel of the kingdom
> will be preached in the whole world as a testi-
> mony to all nations, and *then the end will come.*"

Most Christians point to this prophecy as a sign that
we are near to the end. The gospel of "love God with all
thy being, and thy neighbor as thyself" has now been
preached across the world.

> Matt. 9:15-33   *"So when you see standing in
> the holy place the abomination that causes
> desolation, spoken of through the prophet
> Daniel—let the reader understand—then let
> those who are in Judea flee to the mountains.
> "Let no one on the roof of his house go down
> to take anything out of the house.
> "Let no one in the field go back to get his cloak.
> "How dreadful it will be in those days for
> pregnant women and nursing mothers!
> "Pray that your flight will not take place in
> winter or on the Sabbath.
> "For then there will be great distress, un-*

equaled from the beginning of the world until now—and never to be equaled again.

"If those days had not been cut short, no one would survive, but for the sake of the elect those days will be shortened.

"At that time if anyone says to you, 'Look, here is the Messiah!' or, 'There he is!' do not believe it.

"For false Messiahs and false prophets will appear and perform great signs and miracles to deceive even the elect—if that were possible.

"See, I have told you ahead of time.

"So if anyone tells you, 'There he is, out in the desert,' do not go out; or, 'Here he is, in the inner rooms,' do not believe it.

"For as lightning that comes from the east is visible even in the west, so will be the coming of the Son of Man.

"Wherever there is a carcass, there the vultures will gather.

"Immediately after the distress of those days the sun will be darkened, and the moon will not give its light; the stars will fall from the sky, and the heavenly bodies will be shaken.

"At that time the sign of the Son of Man will appear in the sky, and all the nations of the earth will mourn. They will see the Son of Man coming on the clouds of the sky, with power and great glory.

"And he will send his angels with a loud trumpet call, and they will gather his elect from the four winds, from one end of the heavens to the other.

"Now learn this lesson from the fig tree: As soon as its twigs get tender and its leaves come out, you know that summer is near.

"Even so, *when you see all these things, you know that it is near, right at the door.*"

Jesus may be referring to the door of our consciousnesses, as well as the door into this world.

Matt. 9:34-35   "I tell you the truth, this generation will certainly not pass away until all these things have happened.

"Heaven and earth will pass away, but my words [logos] will never pass away."

Jesus is using the Greek word "logos" instead of "lalia" for "word." Logos means more than word. It means the central essence of being.

Matt. 9:36-39   "No one knows about that day or hour, not even the angels in heaven, nor the Son, but only the Father.

"As it was in the days of Noah, so it will be at the coming of the Son of Man.

"For in the days before the flood, people were eating and drinking, marrying and giving in marriage, up to the day Noah entered the ark; and they understood nothing about what would happen until the flood came and took them all away. *That is how it will be at the coming of the Son of Man."*

There are several indications that Jesus is speaking about the inner and outer worlds and forces. The dire descriptions make it sound impossible to live through this coming birth: " . . . there will be great distress, unequaled from the beginning of the world until now—and never to be equaled again." And, "If those days had not been cut short, no one would survive, but for the sake of the elect those days will be shortened." If you've ever watched a woman give birth, then you know how impossible it all seems. When asked how any can be saved, Jesus answered, "With man it is impossible, but with God all things are possible."

Individuals and the world may seem to be dying in a whirl of fire and flood, but the spirit and God will be delivered and reign for ever and ever. We will not die, but all will be changed.

> Rev. 21:1-6 *Then I saw a new heaven and a new earth, for the first heaven and the first earth had passed away, and there was no longer any sea.*
>
> I saw the Holy City, the new Jerusalem, coming down out of heaven from God, prepared as a bride beautifully dressed for her husband.
>
> And I heard a loud voice from the throne saying, *"Now the dwelling of God is with men, and he will live with them. They will be his people, and God himself will be with them and be their God.*
>
> *"He will wipe every tear from their eyes. There will be no more death or mourning or crying or pain, for the old order of things has passed away."*
>
> He who was seated on the throne said, "I am making everything new!" Then he said, "Write this down, for these words are trustworthy and true."
>
> He said to me: "It is done. I am the Alpha and the Omega, *the Beginning and the End.* To him who is thirsty I will give to drink freely from the spring of the Water of Life."

Certainly, the End Times' prophecies in the Bible are something to be seriously considered. They include a war greater than any yet fought on earth, an earthquake larger than any experienced on earth and many other serious challenges to physical life as we know it. However, woven through all these terrible events is a thread of light that leads us to "the glory that was ours before the world was."

2

The Prophecies
of Edgar Cayce

I n the mid 1920s to 1944, Edgar Cayce produced
more material on the End Times and Earth Changes
than any other source I know of. The volume of material is staggering. But what is more important is
that much of the material is very specific to what will
happen and when.

Edgar Cayce (pronounced KAY-see) was born on a
farm near Hopkinsville, Kentucky, on March 18, 1877. As
a child he displayed unusual powers of perception. At
the age of six he told his parents that he could see and
talk with "visions," sometimes of relatives who had recently died, and even angels. He could also sleep with
his head on his schoolbooks and awake with a photo-
graphic recall of their contents, even sighting the page

upon which the answer appeared. However, after completing seventh grade he left school—which was not unusual for boys at that time.

When he was twenty-one, he developed a paralysis of the throat muscles which caused him to lose his voice. When doctors were unable to find a physical cause for this condition, Edgar Cayce asked a friend to help him re-enter the same kind of hypnotic sleep that had enabled him to memorize his schoolbooks as a child. The friend gave him the necessary suggestions, and once he was in this trance state, Cayce spoke clearly and directly without any difficulty. He instructed the hypnotist to give him a suggestion to increase the bloodflow to his throat; when the suggestion was given, Cayce's throat turned blood red. Then, while still under hypnosis, Cayce recommended some specific medication and manipulative therapy which would aid and, in fact, did aid in restoring his voice completely.

On subsequent occasions, Cayce would go into the hypnotic state to diagnose and prescribe healing for others, with much success. Doctors around Hopkinsville and Bowling Green, Kentucky, took advantage of Cayce's unique talent to diagnose their patients. They soon discovered that all Cayce needed was the name and address of a patient to "tune in" telepathically to that individual's mind and body. The patient didn't have to be near Cayce, he could tune in to them wherever they were.

When one of the young M.D.s working with Cayce submitted a report on his strange abilities to a clinical research society in Boston, the reactions were amazing. On October 9, 1910, The *New York Times* carried two pages of headlines and pictures. From then on, people from all over the country sought the "sleeping prophet," as he was to become known.

The routine he used for conducting a trance-diagnosis was to recline on a couch, hands folded across his solar plexus, and breathe deeply. Eventually, his eyelids would begin fluttering and his breathing would become deep and rhythmical. This was the signal to the conductor (usually his wife, Gertrude) to make verbal contact with Cayce's subconscious by giving a suggestion. Unless this procedure was timed to synchronize with his fluttering eyelids and the change in his breathing, Cayce would proceed beyond his trance state and simply fall fast asleep. However, once the suggestion was made, Cayce would proceed to describe the patient as though he or she were sitting right next to him, his mind functioning much as an x-ray scanner, seeing into every organ of their body. When he was finished, he would say, "Ready for questions." However, in many cases his mind would have already anticipated the patient's questions, answering them during the main session. Eventually, he would say, "We are through for the present," whereupon the conductor would give the suggestion to return to normal consciousness.

If this procedure was in any way violated, Cayce was in serious personal danger. On one occasion, he remained in a trance state for three days and had actually been given up for dead by the attending doctors.

At each session a stenographer (usually Gladys Davis Turner, his personal secretary) would record everything Cayce said. Sometimes during a trance session Cayce would even correct the stenographer's spelling. It was as though his mind was in touch with everything around him and beyond.

Each client was identified with a number to keep their names private. For example, hypnotic material for Edgar Cayce himself is filed under the number 294. His first "reading," as they were called, would be numbered 294-1, and each subsequent reading would increase the dash number (294-2, 294-3, and so on). Some numbers refer to groups of people, such as the Study Group, 262, and some numbers refer to specific research or guidance readings, such as the 254 series containing "the work" readings dealing with the overall work of the organization that grew up around him, and the 364 and 996 series containing the readings on Atlantis.

It was August 10, 1923, before anyone thought to ask the "sleeping" Cayce for insights beyond physical health—questions about life, death, and human destiny. In a small hotel room in Dayton, Ohio, Arthur Lammers asked the first set of philosophical questions that were to lead to an entirely new way of using Cayce's strange abilities. It was during this line of questioning that Cayce first began to talk about reincarnation as though it were as real and natural as the functionings of a physical body. This shocked and challenged Cayce and his family. They were deeply religious people, doing this work to help others because that's what their Christian faith taught. Reincarnation was not part of their reality. Yet, the healings and help continued to come. So, the Cayce family continued with the physical material, but cautiously reflected on the strange philosophical material. Ultimately, the Cayce's began to accept the ideas, though not as reincarnation per se. Edgar Cayce preferred to call it, "The Continuity of Life." He read the Bible every year, from front to back, and felt that it did contain much evidence that life, the true life in the Spirit, was continual.

Eventually, Edgar Cayce, following advice from his own readings moved to Virginia Beach, Virginia, and set up a hospital where he continued to conduct his "Physical Readings" for the health of others. But he also continued this new line of readings called "Life Readings." From 1925 through 1944 he conducted some 2,500 of these Life Readings, describing the past lives of individuals as casually as if everyone understood reincarnation was a reality. Such subjects as deep-seated fears, mental blocks, vocational talents, innate urges and abilities, marriage difficulties, child training, etc., were examined in the light of what the readings called the "karmic patterns" resulting from previous lives spent by the individual's soul on the earth plane.

When he died on January 3, 1945, in Virginia Beach, he left well over 14,000 documented stenographic records of the telepathic-clairvoyant readings he had given for more than 6,000 different people over a period of forty-three years.

The readings constitute one of the largest and most impressive records of psychic perception. Together with their relevant records, correspondence and reports, they have been cross-indexed under thousands of subject headings and placed at the disposal of doctors, psychologists, students, writers, and investigators who still come to examine them. Of course, they are also available to the general public in topical books or complete volumes of the readings, even on CD ROM for DOS, MacIntosh, and Windows software.

A foundation known as the Association for Research and Enlightenment (A.R.E.) was founded in 1932 to preserve these readings. As an open-membership research society, it continues to index and catalog the information, initiate investigation and experiments, and conduct conferences, seminars and lectures. The A.R.E. also has the largest and finest library of parapsychological and metaphysical books in the world.[1]

THE PROBLEM INTERPRETING HIS READINGS

Edgar Cayce's readings do present some difficulties in interpretation and understanding. First, they are somewhat difficult to read, mostly due to their syntax and the presence of arcaic or biblical terms and style. They are *written* records of a *verbal* presentation, a process that occasionally does not carry the full intent that was expressed, and punctuation can significantly change the meaning or intent of the voiced statement. Also, most of the readings were given to specific people with uniquely personal perspectives and prejudices on the topics being discussed, and therefore, the responses were slanted to fit the seeker's perspective. For example, in a reading for one person, Cayce recommends one marriage for life, to another he recommends never getting married and to a third he encourages him to marry at least twice. In the few cases where a reading was purposefully for broader presentation to many people, even the masses, the "sleeping" Cayce was still somewhat at the mercy and wisdom of the those directing the session and asking the questions. Nevertheless, Cayce and his wife Gertrude and their assistant Gladys were very conscientious people, always seeking to be exact and true to the original intent of the reading. As I indicated earlier, the "sleeping" Cayce would occasionally stop his direct discourse to give an aside to Gladys about the way she was recording the material, correcting spelling or giving a clarifying explanation of something he had just said. Finally, because some of Cayce's readings cover so many points or issues within the text, it can be difficult to determine which one he is referring to when the paragraphs are so complex. Despite all of this, with practice, one can become familiar enough with the syntax, terms and "thys," "thees," "thous," a repetitive use of the word "that," and the complex thought pattern, that one can learn to read and understand the Cayce readings fairly easily. Still, I have been in situations when experienced readers of Cayce's work can read the same readings and come up with differing views as to what they mean.

For example, on this topic of End Times and Earth Changes, there are differing views within A.R.E. as to just what is going to happen, if anything. Some believe that the Cayce readings have predicted earth changes that simply have not occurred; in other words, he was wrong, and could therefore be wrong about everything. Others say that these readings were misinterpreted, and the changes spoken of are yet to come. Some believe that there are Cayce readings that say the earth changes are all subject to modification or even suspension of their prophesied outcome if humanity makes some changes in their hearts and minds. Others believe Cayce's readings state that some earth changes are virtual actualities waiting for their time to manifest, simply a matter of destiny. The sheer volume and complexity of the material makes if difficult for everyone to agree on what is in the readings and what they mean. I hope I can clarify some of this for all our sakes.

Most of the Cayce readings presented in this book are edited for clarity, readability and focus to the point at hand. However, I've included all the reading numbers so you can review the originals, if you wish. When Cayce was engaged with a specific person in what amounts to a mind-to-mind discussion or even debate about these issues, I have attempted to show the whole of that discussion/debate, even when it covers several issues beyond the End Times and Earth Changes. I believe this gives us a better understanding of the overall context of the reading.

EDGAR CAYCE PROPHECIES

Since there has been some debate over the quality of the earth-change readings given through the sleeping Cayce by an entity called "Halaliel," I have deliberately kept these readings by themselves, and will begin with them.

Earth Changes as Conveyed Through Cayce
by Halaliel

Halaliel (pronounced, Ha-la-lee-EL) first identified himself through the sleeping Cayce on October 15, 1933, during a Study Group reading on the lesson titled, "Day and Night." There had been 55 readings given to this Study Group. Occasionally, messages had come through the sleeping Cayce from other entities in the spirit realms, but never was the complete reading credited to a single spirit entity. The reading began and continued as usual, but it ended on a strange note. Here is the last question of this reading and the answer given.

Q: Comment upon the following. Does it carry any light of truth?

The Creator, in seeking to create a being worthy of companionship, realized that such a being would result only from having free will and exercising its divine inheritance through its own efforts to find its Maker. Thus, making the choice really a Divine one has caused the existence of states of consciousness, that would indeed tax the free will of a soul; thus light and darkness. Truly, only those tried so as by fire can enter in.

A: The only variation that we would make is that all souls in the beginning were *one* with the Father. The separation, or turning away, brought evil. Then there became the necessity of the awareness of self's being out of accord with blessedness, or out of the realm of blessedness; and, as given of the Son, "yet learned he obedience through the things which he suffered."

COME, my children! Ye no doubt have gained from the comment this day, a *new initiate has*

spoken in or through this channel; Halaliel,
that was with those in the beginning who
warred with those that separated themselves
and became as naught. [my italics] (262-56)

The closing line is referring to the legendary battle
between the angels of rebellion, led by Lucifer, and the
angels of light, led by Michael. Apparently, Halaliel was
among those angels of light that warred with the separating angels, who later became known as the Fallen Angels.

The next time Halaliel is mentioned by the sleeping
Cayce is on October 24, 1933, at the morning reading.
This time the reading is a "research reading" dealing with
the subjects of psychic phenomena, spiritism, and spir-
itualism. The reading ends very strangely again, giving a
list of entities who can be of help in gaining a better understanding of these concepts, instructing the conductor (Gertrude Cayce, Edgar's wife) to call these "forces"
to be present for the next reading.

> The forces gathered here may be used in gain-
> ing this concept. As ye seek, ask first if all these
> are present: Lamech, Confucius, Tamah, Halaliel,
> Hebe, Ra, Ra-Ta, John. (5756-10)

That very afternoon, at the 3:00 p.m. reading, Gertrude
began the reading in accord with the morning suggestion.

> GC (Gertrude Cayce): If the "forces" Lamech,
> Confucius, Tamah, Halaliel, Hebe, Ra, Ra-Ta,
> John are present, we seek the answer to the fol-
> lowing question. (5756-11)

Gladys' notes at the end of this reading include this

statement: "Edgar Cayce said on waking that he would like to always feel surrounded by as helpful influences as he did this time."

On January 7, 1934, the 57th Study Group reading was given and one of those in attendance asked, "Who is Halaliel?" Here's the answer:

> One in and with whose courts Ariel fought when there was the rebellion in heaven. Now, where is heaven? Where is Ariel, and who was he? A companion of Lucifer or Satan, and one that made for the disputing of the influences in the experiences of Adam in the Garden. (262-57)

Clearly we are dealing with the legendary war of the angels. All the angels were originally created in the image of the Creator, but through the misuse of free will some rebelled against the cooperative spirit of Oneness. This rebellion would not be allowed; it was like a cancer in the Universal Consciousness. So, they were driven from heaven until such time that they repented of their self-seeking ways and re-attuned themselves to the Creator's harmonious spirit of oneness. Notice that the literal meanings of their names are quite beautiful and powerful, as they were originally intended to be: Ariel means "lion of God" and Lucifer means "light giver." The name Satan is actually from a Hebrew word that simply means "adversary." This is why the Messiah is often called the "advocate;" he is our counter-influence to the adversary.

At the end of this reading, Gladys noted that Edgar Cayce had a slightly different experience during the reading. Normally, he would go to the Hall of Records to receive the Book of Life (the records) of the individual for whom the reading was being given. This time he felt that a "group activity" took place in the back of the building where he received the records. Could this have been the group of Lamech, Confucius, Tamah, Halaliel, Hebe, Ra, Ra-Ta, and John?

The very next time Halaliel is mentioned is on the 8th of January, 1934, in a reading for a female society leader and Theosophist, No. 443. She had been asking a series of very involved questions about mysticism and spiritual truth, then she asked:

> Q: How high is the source that this information is being given from?
> A: From the universal forces, and as emanated through the teacher that gives same—as one that has been given—Halaliel. (443-3)

A few days later, on the 19th, we get the first earth changes material delivered by Halaliel, or at least some portion of the reading was from Halaliel because he says so in the midst of the reading. This whole reading is unusual. For the first time they are using a recording instrument to record the reading. Instead of Gertrude conducting, their eldest son, Hugh Lynn Cayce was the conductor, and in his opening suggestion to Edgar, he instructs Edgar to stop every fifteen minutes so the recording device can be reloaded. Amazingly, the sleeping Edgar stops exactly every fifteen minutes throughout the reading, even if he is in mid-sentence. Here is Hugh Lynn's opening suggestion and the sleeping Edgar's response:

> HLC: We seek at this time such information as will be of value and interest to those present regarding the spiritual, mental, and physical changes which are coming to the earth. You will tell us what part we may play in meeting

and helping others to understand these changes.
At the end of each fifteen minute period you
will pause, until I tell you to continue, while the
recording instrument is being arranged. You
will speak distinctly at a normal rate of speech,
and you will answer the questions which we
ask.

EC: Yes; as each of you gathered here have
your own individual development, yet as each
seeks to be a channel of blessings to the fellow
man, each attunes self to the Throne of universal information. And, there may be accorded
you that which may be beneficial, not only in
thine own experience, but that which will
prove helpful, hopeful, in the experience of
others. (3976-15)

From here the reading goes into a brief description of
the number and nature of the spirit entities that are
gathered about them now to help with this reading.
Then, the reading tells of the return of one of their members to the earth to help with this coming period of earth
changes. The returning entity is the disciple John the
Beloved. Then the reading begins to address the coming
earth changes. Remember, the reading is being given in
January of 1934.

As to the material changes that are to be as
an omen, as a sign to those that this is shortly
to come to pass—as has been given of old, the
sun will be darkened and the earth shall be
broken up in divers places[2]—and THEN shall
be PROCLAIMED—through the spiritual inter-
ception in the hearts and minds and souls of
those that have sought His way—that HIS star
has appeared, and will point the way for *those*

that enter into the holy of holies in themselves.
For, God the Father, God the Teacher, God the
director, in the minds and hearts of men, must
ever be IN those that come to know Him as first
and foremost in the seeking of those souls; for
He is first the GOD to the individual and as He
is exemplified, as He is manifested in the heart
and in the acts of the body of the individual,
then He becomes manifested before men. And
those that seek in the latter portion of the year
of our Lord (as ye have counted in and among
men) '36, He will appear. [my italics] (3976-15)

My italics make the phrase that fits so well with the
Daniel visions. Recall that one of Daniel's items was entering the sanctuary, the holy of holies within each of us.
Here Halaliel speaks to the same activity, saying that
those who do go within their sanctuary will know, will be
guided. The "He will appear" phrase is developed further
elsewhere in the Cayce readings. Cayce says that the
Messiah (Christ) first comes in the hearts and minds of
those that seek this influence, then it moves into the
physical realm, ultimately becoming fully manifest, as
we are, incarnate. Cayce says, "He will walk and talk with
people of every clime." (364-13) Here Halaliel is stating
that the beginning of this process is in 1936, for those
that seek within themselves. Then Halaliel continues, focusing on earth changes:

As to the changes physical again: The earth
will be broken up in the western portion of
America. The greater portion of Japan must go
into the sea. The upper portion of Europe will
be changed as in the twinkling of an eye. Land
will appear off the east coast of America. There
will be the upheavals in the Arctic and in the

Antarctic that will make for the eruption of vol-
canos in the Torrid areas [areas between the
Tropic of Cancer and the Tropic of Capricorn
divided by the equator], and there will be shifting then of the poles—so that where there has
been those of a frigid or the semitropical will
become the more tropical, and moss and fern
will grow. And these will *begin* in those periods
in '58 to '98, when these will be proclaimed as
the periods when His light will be seen again
in the clouds. As to times, as to seasons, as to
places, ALONE is it given to those who have
named the name—and who bear the mark of
those of His calling and His election in their
bodies. To them it shall be given.

As to those things that deal with the mental
of the earth, these shall call upon the mountains to cover many. As ye have seen those in
lowly places raised to those of power in the
political, in the machinery of nations' activities, so shall ye see those in high places re-
duced and calling on the waters of darkness to
cover them. And those that in the inmost recesses of theirselves awaken to the spiritual
truths that are to be given, and those places
that have acted in the capacity of teachers
among men, the rottenness of those that have
ministered in places will be brought to light,
and turmoils and strifes shall enter. And, as
there is the wavering of those that would enter
as emissaries, as teachers, from the throne of
life, the throne of light, the throne of immortality, and wage war in the air with those of
darkness, then know ye the Armageddon is at
hand. For with the great numbers of the gath-
ering of the hosts of those that have hindered

> and would make stumbling blocks for man
> and his weaknesses, they shall wage war with
> the spirits of light that come into the earth for
> this awakening; that have been and are being
> called by those of the sons of men into the ser-
> vice of the living God. For He, as ye have been
> told, is not the God of the dead, not the God of
> those that have forsaken Him, but those that
> love His coming, that love His associations
> among men—the God of the LIVING, the God
> of Life! For, He IS Life. (3976-15)

At this point, the reading shifts back to the return of
John the Beloved, whose name is stated as "John Peniel"
(pronounced, pen-ee-EL). Of course, "peniel" means
"face of God" in Hebrew, and was the name Jacob gave
to the place where he met God face-to-face and his own
name was changed to Israel, which means "strives with
God." The reading says that John will be known in
America by those that have gone through the regenera-
tion in their bodies, minds and spirits, and that he will
give "the new order of things." John will be able to make
these things "PLAIN in the minds of men, that they may
know the truth, the life, the light, will make them free."
Then the reading goes into an intense, inspiring call to
awaken, filled with biblical phrases and ending with
Halaliel identifying himself as the deliverer of this information:

> I have declared this, that has been delivered
> unto me to give unto you, ye that sit here and
> that hear and that see a light breaking in the
> east, and have heard, have seen thine weak-
> nesses and thine faultfindings, and know that
> He will make thy paths straight if ye will but
> live that YE KNOW this day. Then, may the next

step, the next word, be declared unto thee. For
ye in your weakness have known the way,
through that as ye have made manifest of the
SPIRIT of truth and light that has been proclaimed into this earth, that has been committed unto the keeping of Him that made of
Himself no estate but who brought into being
all that ye see manifest in the earth. He has declared this message unto thee: "Love the Lord
thy God with all thine heart," and the second is
like unto it, "Love thy neighbor as thyself." Who
is thine neighbor? Him that ye may aid in
whatsoever way that he, thy neighbor, thy
brother, has been troubled. Help him to stand
on his own feet. For such may only know the
acceptable way. The weakling, the unsteady,
must enter into the crucible and become as
naught, even as He, that they may know the
way. I, Halaliel, have spoken. (3976-15)

This is followed by a series of questions from the par-
ticipants. The first question deals directly with the earth
changes, and it is here that Halaliel begins to get into
trouble with future students of this material. They point
out that the first question asked what earth changes
would occur "this year"; that would have been 1934. But
the answer clearly does not address 1934, nor did any of
the changes mentioned occur in '34. Perhaps Halaliel's
consciousness was too vast to focus on '34, or '34 never
made a sufficient impact on his consciousness to get a
specific answer, and so Halaliel keeps on discussing the
earth changes as a whole, over many years to come. Perhaps the initial suggestion to give information about any
earth changes was still the dominant suggestion, and
Hugh Lynn did not sufficiently emphasize that he now
only wanted changes that would physically occur in

1934. Whatever the reason, it is clear that Halaliel did not focus on 1934:

> Q: What are the world changes to come this year physically?
> A: The earth will be broken up in many places. The early portion will see a change in the physical aspect of the west coast of America. There will be open waters in the northern portions of Greenland. There will be new lands seen off the Caribbean Sea, and DRY land will appear. There will be the falling away in India of much of the material suffering that has been brought on a troubled people. There will be the reduction of one risen to power in central Europe to naught. The young king son will soon reign [in Germany]. In America in the political forces we see a restabilization of the powers of the peoples in their own hands, a breaking up of the rings, the cliques in many places. South America shall be shaken from the uppermost portion to the end, and in the Antarctic off of Tierra del Fuego LAND, and a strait with rushing waters. (3976-15)

Earlier in this reading you'll notice that the earth changes are to "*begin* in those periods '58—'98." I believe that Halaliel's consciousness was still filled with this information, and continued to reveal to us the overall sequence of the changes. Now Hugh Lynn shifts the topic to political issues dealing with 1934 in Germany and America with a series of questions. Then, he ends with an open question for any more advice, and we get this:

> Q: Is there any further counsel or advice for

us gathered here, which will enable us to understand better our responsibility?

A: All gathered here in the name of God who is the Father, to those that seek to know His ways—and who is as something outside the veil of their understanding *unless sought!* The counsel of the Father, of that God-Mother comes in each soul that seeks to know the biddings; not as one that would reap vengeance but rather as the loving, MERCIFUL Father. For, as ye show mercy, so may the Father show mercy to thee. As ye show the wisdom, as ye show the love of thy fellow man, so may the love be shown, so may the wisdom, so may the guiding steps day-by-day be shown thee. Be ye joyous in the Lord, knowing that He is ever present with those that seek His face. He is not in heaven, but makes heaven in thine own heart, if ye accept Him. He, God, the Father, is present and manifest in that ye mete to your fellow man in thine own experience.

Would ye know the Father, be the father to thy brother. Would ye know the love of the Father, SHOW thy love to thy faltering, to thy erring brother—but to those that seek, not those that condemn.

We are through. (3976-15)

I simply cannot throw this material out because Halaliel did not correctly address the 1934 physical earth changes question! There is simply too much in this reading that is obviously from a very high source of attunement and guidance. I do not see Halaliel exalting himself or attempting to attract attention to himself. He seems to be directing everyone's attention to God, God within themselves, exactly what Jesus encouraged. The false prophets that Jesus warned us about were those that said Messiah is over here or there rather than within us. Halaliel is saying exactly what Jesus taught, "the kingdom of heaven is within you." These earth change prophecies should not be ignored because he missed the focusing question about "this year."

Halaliel continues to make appearances in the readings over the next several months of 1934. On the 9th of September, the Study Group met again for its 71st reading and they believed that they had received further information about Halaliel, though it is not clearly stated as such in the reading. Here's what they heard and assumed to be referring to Halaliel:

> TO ALL WE WOULD GIVE: Be patient. That part thou hast chosen in such a work is born of truth. Let it come in and be a part of thy daily life. Look in upon the experiences, for, as will be seen, my children, *there has been appointed one that may aid thee in thy future lessons, and he will be thy teacher, thy guide, one sent through the power of thine own desires.* Thine own selves, then, may present his being, meeting, living, dwelling, with thee. *Not the Christ, but His messenger, with the Christ from the beginning, and is to other worlds what the Christ is to this earth.* [my italics] (262-71)

Some in the Study Group, including Hugh Lynn Cayce, wanted to reject Halaliel's help, fearful that they might be led away from Christ. They ultimately did reject his help and asked that only the Christ guide them. Gladys notes that "two or three in the group were still not convinced that we were right in rejecting Halaliel's help in preparing the lessons." Whatever the truth about Halaliel, we hear nothing from him again, and his earth changes comments are often questioned by those that feel he was not a high source, despite the reading's comments to the contrary. Fortunately, we have many other Cayce readings on earth changes that support and enhance Halaliel's prophecies.

Other Earth Changes Readings by Cayce

This first one occurs on January 21, 1936, two years after the Halaliel readings. Basically, it is a personal reading for Mr. 270, dealing with many personal issues, but toward the end of the reading, Mr. 270 asks the following question:

> Q: What is the primary cause of earthquakes? Will San Francisco suffer from such a catastrophe this year [1936]? If so, give date, time and information for the guidance of this body, who has personal property, records and a wife, all of which it wishes safety.
>
> A: We do not find that this particular district (San Francisco) in the present year ['36] will suffer the great MATERIAL damages that HAVE been experienced heretofore. While portions of the country will be affected, we find these will be farther EAST than San Francisco—or those SOUTH, where there has NOT been heretofore the greater activity.
>
> The causes of earthquakes, of course, are the movements of the earth; that is, internally. And, the cosmic activity or influence of other planetary forces and stars produce the activities of the elementals of the earth; that is, the Earth, the Air, the Fire, the Water—and those combinations make for the replacements in the various activities.
>
> If there are the greater activities in the

Vesuvius, or Pelée, then the southern coast of California—and the areas between Salt Lake and the southern portions of Nevada—may expect, within the three months following the greater activity, an inundation by the earthquakes. But these, as we find, are to be more in the southern than in the northern hemisphere.

We are through for the present. (270-35)

This fits very well with Halaliel's prophecy, "The earth will be broken up in the western portion of America." It also fits with a dream that Edgar Cayce had, and subsequently gave a reading on. Here it is:

Dream. 3/3/36 on train from Detroit to Va. Beach.

The dream was:

I had been born again in 2158 A.D. in Nebraska. The sea apparently covered all of the western part of the country, as the city where I lived was on the coast. The family name was a strange one. At an early age as a child I declared myself to be Edgar Cayce who had lived 200 yrs. before. Scientists, men with long beards, little hair, and thick glasses, were called in to observe me. They decided to visit the places where I said I had been born, lived and worked, in Ky., Ala., N.Y., Mich., and Va. Taking me with them, the group of scientists visited these places in a long, cigar-shaped, metal flying ship which moved at high speed. Water covered part of Alabama. Norfolk, Va. had become an immense seaport. N.Y. had been destroyed either by war or an earthquake and was being rebuilt. Industries were scattered

over the countryside. Most of the houses were
of glass. Many records of my work as Edgar
Cayce were discovered and collected. The
group returned to Nebraska taking the records
with them to study. (294-185)

Some researchers say that this is only a dream, and
should therefore not be taken too seriously. But it isn't
just a dream. A Cayce reading was given on the dream at
the Fifth Congress of the A.R.E., and the reading clearly
supports the dream's images as images of actual earth
changes to come. However, the reading also gives clear
instructions to those of us living prior to the changes or
in the midst of them: "That the periods from the material angle as visioned are to come to pass matters not to
the soul, but do thy duty TODAY! TOMORROW will care
for itself." And, "Make thy will one with His. Be not
afraid." Here's the reading:

Q: Interpret and explain the dream which
Edgar Cayce had on March 3, 1936, in which
he was born again over two hundred years in
the future and traveled to various sections of
this country where records of Edgar Cayce
could be found.
A: This then is the interpretation. As has
been given, "Fear not." Keep the faith; for those
that be with thee are greater than those that
would hinder. Though the very heavens fall,
though the earth shall be changed, though the
heavens shall pass, the promises in Him are
sure and will stand—as in that day—as the
proof of thy activity in the lives and hearts of
those of thy fellow man.
For indeed and in truth ye know, "As ye do it
unto thy fellow man, ye do it unto thy God, to

thyself." For, SELF effaced, God may indeed glorify thee and make thee STAND as one that is called for a purpose in the dealings, the relationships with thy fellow man.

Be not unmindful that He is nigh unto thee in every trial, in every temptation, and hath not willed that thou shouldest perish.

Make thy will then one with His. Be not afraid.

That is the interpretation. That the periods from the material angle as visioned are to come to pass matters not to the soul, but do thy duty TODAY! TOMORROW will care for itself.

These changes in the earth will come to pass, for the time and times and half times are at an end, and there begin those periods for the readjustments. For how hath He given? "The righteous shall inherit the earth."

Hast thou, my brethren, a heritage in the earth? (294-185)

This reading clearly states that the scenes in the dream are "changes in the earth that will come to pass, for the time and times and half times are at an end"—a reference to Daniel's prophecy. The reading goes on to say that these changes "begin those periods [of] readjustments," indicating that the readjustments will fulfill the prophecy that "the righteous shall inherit the earth" (Matt. 5:10).

Obviously, the Cayce readings are predicting significant changes for America; most drastic changes will be in South America, but North America will have its share. The changes to the western coast of North America are apparently triggered by the two volcanoes, Vesuvius in Italy and Pelée on the island of Martinique in the West Indies.

In 1941 Cayce gave another detailed description of the prophesied earth changes.

> As to conditions in the geography of the world, of the country, changes are gradually coming about.
>
> In the next few years lands will appear in the Atlantic as well as in the Pacific. And what is the coastline of many a land now will be the bed of the ocean. Even many of the battlefields of the present [1941 WW II] will be ocean, will be the seas, the bays, the lands over which the *new* order will carry on their trade.
>
> Portions of the now east coast of New York, or New York City itself, will disappear. This will be another generation though. The southern portions of Carolina, Georgia will disappear [Could he be referring to movement along the major fault in Charlestown, S.C.?]. This will come first.
>
> The waters of the lakes [Great Lakes] will empty into the Gulf [of Mexico] rather than the waterway over which such discussions have been recently made [St. Lawrence Seaway]. It would be well if the new waterway were prepared.
>
> Then the area where the entity is now located [Virginia Beach] will be among the safety lands, as will be what is now Ohio, Indiana and Illinois and much of the southern portion of Canada and the eastern portion of Canada. While, the western land is to be disturbed. (1152-11)

Ms. 1152 finishes this reading with some very direct questions about New York City, Los Angeles, and San Francisco.

Q: I have for many months felt that I should move away from New York City.

A: This is well. There is too much unrest. There will continue to be the character of vibrations that to this body will be disturbing. Eventually, there will be the destructive forces there—though these will be in the next generation.

Q: Will Los Angeles be safe?

A: Los Angeles, San Francisco, most all of these will be among those that will be destroyed before New York even. (1152-11)

In 1942 a person asks if their business location would be safe until their lease expires. The answer was that those locations on the mainland would be safe but not those on Manhattan Island [412-13]. The trouble with this reading is that the lease in question was for only one year, expiring in 1943, and Manhattan Island is still there. Is this another example of a vision of the future affecting Cayce's deeper consciousness so profoundly that it cannot relate to the one-year time frame of the question? Or, is it simply a mistake?

The Supply and Demand for Food

The previous few readings may give a sense of specific changes in the physical structure to portions of North America, but the next few readings indicate that the extreme hardships prophesied will actually come to the country as a whole. For example, in 1942 Mr. 416 asks if he should hold onto his lots and acreage in Virginia Beach, or sell. The sleeping Cayce tells him to sell the lots and hold onto the acreage because it will be needed to grow food for himself and those closely associated with him during "the extreme periods through which all portions of the country must pass." [416-17] Since this warning is certainly *after* the Great Depression, we can assume that another cycle of difficulty with the material necessities of life is coming. As of yet, this is 1994, we have seen no evidence of any problems with food excepting specific locations where hurricanes, earthquakes, fires, and floods have destroyed the network of modern life's services. In reading 257-254 given in 1943, Cayce responds to a question about the expected changes in America with this answer: "These conditions have not changed. The hardships with the supply and demand for foods in this country have not begun yet." In 1944, in reading 3620-1, he says "Anyone who can buy a farm is fortunate and buy it if you don't want to grow hungry in some days to come."

The Great Pole Shift of 2000 A.D.

In the Halaliel reading that dealt so clearly and specifically with coming earth changes a reference was made to a shifting of the poles. Halaliel said that the changes would begin during the period between 1958 and 1998, but he did not say exactly when the pole shift would occur. In a life reading for Mr. 826 in 1936, Cayce gives a more exact dating. Still, the implication in both Halaliel readings in '34 and this one in '36 is that the pole shift is a developing event over a period of some years, beginning in the '58-'98 range and culminating in the actual shifting in 2000 to 2001.

> Q: What great change or the beginning of what change, if any, is to take place in the earth in the year 2000 to 2001 A.D.?
> A: When there is a shifting of the poles. Or, a new cycle begins. (826-8)

Pole shifts are not new to the earth. Our geologists have evidence that magnetic pole shifts have occurred about every 50,000 years or so. A magnetic pole shift would cause some tremendous problems with communications and weather, but not necessarily a lot of physical destruction. However, during the magnetic shift we could assume that the Van Allen Belts that surround our planet would temporarily breakdown or disappear until a realignment of the new magnetic pattern was established. This could be very harmful to life on the planet. The Van Allen Belts are magnetic fields that surround the earth, channeling incoming radiation from space toward our poles, keeping it from coming into our main living areas on the planet. The luminous bands of the Aurora Borealis (Northern Lights) and the Aurora Australis (Southern Lights) are the visual signs of these magnetic waves coming down through our atmosphere near our northern and southern poles. It is believed that as a magnetic shift began the Belts would have to breakup for a time, perhaps a few hours, a few days, a few months or a few years, until the new magnetic poles were established. Then, presumably the Belts would reestablish their magnetic field around the planet, channeling the incoming radiation to the new poles. During this period the earth would be exposed to increased levels of radiation. Perhaps this is the "fire" that so many prophecies speak of.

If, on the other hand, the pole shift is not simply magnetic, but is a true physical changing of the poles—in other words, the physical planet becomes unstable on its present axis, eventually rolls over and establishes a new axis—then there would very likely be destruction to the tectonic plates, seas, weather patterns, and of course, life forms. Unfortunately, there is one Cayce reading that seems to be talking about an axis shift. However, once again it is a question about the year 1936, and the answer certainly seems to be dealing with a period long beyond '36. Furthermore, it is not a clear statement about the earth's axis shifting.

Q: What will be the type and extent of the upheaval in '36?

A: The wars, the upheavals in the interior of the earth, and the shifting of same *by the differentiation in the axis* as respecting the positions from the Polaris center. [my italics] (5748-6)

This statement is in the midst of a reading on ancient Egypt and the Great Pyramid, which we will look at more closely later on. According to Cayce, and many researchers, the opening to the Great Pyramid faces toward the North Star, Polaris. In this reading and others, Cayce indicates that the Dipper is changing its shape (which it has been doing for many thousands of years) and that when the change is so significant that we notice it, the opening to the Great Pyramid will align to Polaris differently. If "the differentiation in the axis" means a change in the earth's axis, then we are talking about a physical pole shift. It seems to say that Polaris will move and so will our axis.

There are plenty of references in the Cayce readings about the poles being opposite in ancient times, especially his readings on ancient Egypt.

One thing we do know about the pole shift, it is prophesied by Cayce to be between the year 2000 and 2001—not too far away. But Cayce sees something happening even sooner.

1998: Cayce's Year of Great Events

The Cayce readings make six references to the year 1998. All six are significant statements. However, as you will see, each is in a different context. Three are in the context of the Ancient Atlantian and Egyptian period being karmically driven into play again during our lives, with the purposes, powers, and souls that were involved then returning to life for another try. Without going into the entire Atlantis/Egypt story, I have tried to include enough of the readings' context to give you the true perspective of the readings. In two of the other three readings, a seeker who is familiar with Jacob Boehme's work is asking the sleeping Cayce a series of questions about the Aquarian Age when she also gets the 1998 date.

Here are the six references to 1998 with their respective reading numbers:

Then began the laying out of the pyramid and the building of same. This had begun in those very mountains where they had taken refuge. It was not only built to remain as a place for receiving offers, just as those in the Temple Beauty where upon various altars an individual's innate self was offered, but to be the place of initiation of the initiates.

The pyramid was formed according to the position of various stars around which this particular solar system circles—*going towards what?* Toward that same place to which the priest [In ancient Egypt, Edgar Cayce had been the priest "RaTa"] was banished—the constellation of Libra, or to Libya were these people sent. Is it not fitting then, that these people must return? As this priest [Edgar Cayce] may develop himself to be in that position to be a LIBERATOR of the world in its relationships to individuals in those periods to come; for he must enter again in that period, or in 1998.

As the changes come about in the earth, those things that were preserved were to later make known in the minds of those peoples to come. The rise and fall of nations were to be depicted in this same temple which acted as an interpreter for that which had been, which is, and

which is to be in the material plane. (294-151)
[my italics]

There are many strange and curious statements in this
reading. I particularly found the comment about "those
things that were preserved were to later make known in
the minds of those peoples to come." In other readings,
Cayce clearly states that we are "those people to come"
and that the images and concepts in the pyramids and
other temples are to help us fully realize who we are and
what we are to be doing. Some of the 19th century investigators of the Pyramids actually did discover a time-line
in the Great Pyramid. That time-line dated from the Fall
from Grace to the year 2033 A.D. At the end of this chapter, I'll go into this in more detail. Let's continue with the
1998 readings:

> The apex of the pyramid (which has long
> since been removed by the sons of Heth [the
> sons of Noah's son Ham in Genesis 10:15] was
> of metal. It was to be indestructible, being of
> copper, brass and gold with other alloys.
> Gizeh was to be the place of the initiates and
> their gaining understanding by personal appli-
> cation and the journeys through various ac-
> tivities in the earth. Then it was fitting that the
> placing of crown on the pyramid, this symbol
> of the record, was done by one who repre-
> sented both the old and the new; one repre-
> senting the Sons of the Law in Atlantis, Lemuria,
> Oz and Og. So, Hept-supht, he who keeps the
> record shut, was chosen as the one to seal that
> in the tomb.
> The old record in Gizeh is from the journey
> to the Pyrenees to the death of the Son of Man,
> as a man, and then to 1998. (378-14)

This last sentence refers to the time-line in the Great Pyramid, which I'll develop at the end of this chapter. But the reference to the Pyrenees is striking because it is also part of the Nostradamus End-Times material and the Divine Feminine's apparitions, many of which occurred in the Pyrenees Mountains. Continuing with the 1998 readings, we have this series of questions:

Q: Is the gradual restoration of phosphorus in man so he will talk back and forth with Cosmos, like the radio principle?

A: This is gradually a development of which the awareness of the use of the spiritual consciousness may be a medium through which such may be done.

Q: What does the restoration of phosphorus signify?

A: The relationship of the individual to that awareness of the Universal Consciousness, which is the promise of all who have wholly put on Him. For as He has given, "he that abideth wholly in me and I in him, to him will be made aware all things from the foundations of the world." This is ALL there, in His words, in His promises to man [John 14 through 17]. Just as indicated in His exhortation upon the revelation activities of John, and as to what they meant in the affairs of man. That place, that awareness. And yet, when individuals will, even as John, become aware of being within the presence of Life itself, God Himself made manifest, how few accepted it?

Q: What will the Aquarian Age mean to mankind as regards Physical, Mental and Spiritual development?

A: These are as growths. In the center of the

Piscean Age we had the entrance of "Emmanuel" or God among men, see? What did that mean? The same will be meant by the full consciousness of the ability to communicate with the Creative Forces, and the uses of same in material environs.

This awareness in the age of Atlantis and Lemuria brought what? The destruction of man, and his beginning of the journey up through selfishness.

Q: Why is the Aquarian Age described as the "Age of the Lily"?

A: The purity. Only the purity as it represents will be able to comprehend or understand that awareness that is before those who seek the way.

Q: Can a date be given to indicate the beginning of the Aquarian Age?

A: It laps over from one to another, as he holds to that which has been, which is—as has been indicated, we will begin to understand fully in '98.

Q: Three hundred years ago Jacob Boehme decreed Atlantis would rise again at this crisis time when we cross from this Piscean Era into the Aquarian. Is Atlantis rising now? Will it cause a sudden convolution and about what year?

A: In 1998 we may find a great deal of the activities as have been wrought by the gradual changes that are coming about. These are at the periods when the cycle of the solar activity, or the years as related to the sun's passage through the various spheres of activity become paramount to the change between the Piscean and the Aquarian age. This is a *gradual*, not a

cataclysmic activity in the experience of the
earth in this period. [my italics] (1602-3)

Ms. 1602 is an amazing seeker, and her questioning of
the sleeping Cayce has brought us some important information. As we shall see, the End Times prophecies
include many comments about our bodies being changed.
Here Ms. 1602 gets Cayce to identify that phosphorus is
rising in our bodies and will someday be sufficient for us
to "become aware of being within the presence of Life
itself, God Himself made manifest." She also gets Cayce
to identify one of the primary qualities of this new era,
saying the last era was "God among men," Cayce says
this coming era will be "the full consciousness of the
ability to communicate with the Creative Forces, and the
uses of same in material environs."

Continuing with the 1998 readings, we have a father
hoping that he and his family can join with Cayce on his
return during this great era:

Q: Will I, or any of my immediate family, re-
incarnate with Mr. Cayce in 1998?
A: This is not to be given, or things of such a
nature, but is to be determined by the desire,
the need, the application of those who may
desire to do so. (2285-1)

Finally, we have a reading that is truly remarkable for
its clear dating of the return of the Messiah. I found it
curious that Cayce chose that term to identify this coming Being. It seems to indicate a universalness to the
coming, rather than the specific religion-connected
term, Christ. Of course, even the Christ said he had
flocks beyond the one he came to. Here's the reading,
again referencing the Great Pyramid and the Xerxes material we discussed in the previous chapter:

In this same pyramid did the Great Initiate, the Master, take those last of the Brotherhood degrees with John, the forerunner of Him, at that place. As is indicated in that period where entrance is shown to be in that land that was set apart, as that promised to that peculiar peoples, as were rejected—as is shown in that portion when there is the turning back from the raising up of Xerxes as the deliverer from an unknown tongue or land, and again is there seen that this occurs in the entrance of the Messiah in this period—1998. (5748-5)

Obviously, the year 1998 is a significant one from Edgar Cayce's perspective. In the Nostradamus material we will see how he viewed 1999 as a key marker. Frankly, these two seers were so close in their timing for a significant change close to the end of the millennium, that a one year variation does not amount to much, in my opinion.

EDGAR CAYCE AND THE END TIMES

As we have seen, the Cayce readings contain many references to the biblical prophecies about the End Times. Perhaps the most amazing one is his bold statement that "the time, times and half times" spoken of in the prophet Daniel's vision are over! Clearly this means that the End Time is upon us. There can be no other interpretation of such a statement. The Edgar Cayce readings repeatedly state that "the time, times and half times" are over.

The Armageddon
The end of the time, times and half times means that a great battle is about to take place between the forces of the light and good and the forces of the darkness and

evil. So, for Cayce, the end of the time, times and half times is the beginning of the last great battle of Armageddon, which will be followed by the thousand years of peace with "Satan bound." You may recall how Halaiel referenced this period in his earth-change reading:

> And those that in the inmost recesses of theirselves awaken to the spiritual truths that are to be given, and those places that have acted in the capacity of teachers among men, the rottenness of those that have ministered in places will be brought to light, and turmoils and strifes shall enter. And, as there is the wavering of those that would enter as emissaries, as teachers, from the throne of life, the throne of light, the throne of immortality, and wage war in the air with those of darkness, *then know ye the Armageddon is at hand.* For with the great numbers of the gathering of the hosts of those that have hindered and would make stumbling blocks for man and his weaknesses, *they shall wage war with the spirits of light that come into the earth for this awakening;* that have been and are being called by those of the sons of men into the service of the living God. For He, as ye have been told, is not the God of the dead, not the God of those that have forsaken Him, but those that love His coming, that love His associations among men—the God of the LIVING, the God of Life! For, He IS Life. [my italics] (3976-15)

There are two more references to the Armageddon in the Cayce readings. One relates to the Great Pyramid in Giza and the other to the spirituality of the American people.

Q: If the Armageddon is foretold in the Great Pyramid, please give a description of it and the date of its beginning and ending.

A: Not in what is left there. *It will be as a thousand years, with the fighting in the air, and—as has been—between those returning to and those leaving the earth.* [my italics] (5748-6)

This certainly fits with the previous reading in which Halaliel describes Armageddon as a battle between "those that would enter as emissaries, as teachers, from the throne of life, the throne of light, the throne of immortality, and wage war in the air with those of darkness." It is also important to note that the Armageddon is to last a thousand years. Hopefully, the end of this war is near, and the thousand years of peace will begin soon.

Reading given in October of 1926
These are rather the conditions as may be expected: The spirituality of the American people will be the criterion of that as is to become the world's forces. As has been given in that of the peace table [Versailles, 1919, ending WW I], there sat the Master in the American people [through President Woodrow Wilson and his group], with the brotherhood of the world accepted—war was at an end. Without same [spirituality and the brotherhood of the world] *there will again come the Armageddon* [WW II?], and in same there will be seen that the Christian forces will AGAIN move westward. [my italics] (900-272)

Here we are in the mid 1990s, the U.S.A. is a survivor of the hot and cold wars of the 1900s, is our spirituality in tact? Do we still hold to the brotherhood of the world?

A Noah-like Time

There is a fascinating reading for a woman who was on Noah's ark, but in the reading Cayce gives some further insights into the coming changes and their relationship to the changes that occurred during Noah's time. You'll recall, even Jesus on the Mt. of Olives references Noah's time. The reading begins with Cayce's mind looking over this woman's "Book of Life," her records on the skein of time and space:

> What an unusual record—and one of those who might be termed as physically the mothers of the world! Because the entity was one of those in Noah's ark.
>
> The entity has appeared when there were new revelations to be given. And again it appears when there are new revelations to be made.
>
> May the entity so conduct its mind, its body, and its purposes, then, as to be a channel through which such messages may come that are needed for the awakenings in the minds of men as to the necessity for returning to the search for their relationship with the Creative Forces or God.
>
> For as has been given from the beginning, the deluge [Noah's flood] was not a myth (as many would have you believe) but a period when man had so belittled himself with the cares of the world, with the deceitfulness of his own knowledge and power, as to require that there be a return to his dependence wholly—physically and mentally—upon the Creative Forces.
>
> Will this entity see such again occur in the earth? Will it be among those who may be given directions as to how, where, the elect

may be preserved for the replenishing again of the earth?

Remember, not by water—for it is the mother of life in the earth—but rather by the elements, fire. (3653-1)

This is a disturbing reading. It seems to be saying that there will be a new destruction, like the one that occurred during Noah's period, yet this time it will be by fire, not water. And it also seems to be saying that the destruction will be of such a magnitude that we'll be "given directions as to how, where, the elect may be preserved for the replenishing again of the earth!"

I know many of us hate these doom prophecies. They are so awesome that it appears impossible to live our daily lives with such a prophecy hanging over our heads. All I can trust in—with my own wife, children and hopes for this life—is Jesus' teaching that with God *all things are possible*. It's also important to realize that this reading does clearly indicate that life will go on, as it did after Noah.

The fire in this reading could possibly come from the increase in radiation as the Van Allen Belts breakdown. This would be "like a fire" and would effect the whole earth.

On the whole, the Cayce readings are positive and encouraging about the future and its potential. They do predict major changes during this next period. Here is a list of the changes predicted in the Cayce readings.

EDGAR CAYCE'S EARTH CHANGES PREDICTIONS

• Much of the West Coast, the Carolina and Georgia southern coast, and the New England coast of the U.S. will be changed.

• Within ninety days of greater activity in either of the two volcanoes Pelée or Vesuvius, powerful earthquakes with cause an inundation in the southern coast of California, and between the Great Salt Lake and southern portions of Nevada.

- Land will rise off the Atlantic and Pacific coasts of the U.S.
- Los Angeles, San Francisco, and eventually New York will be destroyed.
- New York will be rebuilt a little west of where it is today.
- The Great Lakes will empty into the Gulf of Mexico.
- The U.S. will experience food shortages.
- Ultimately, Livingston, Montana, will be one of the breadbaskets of the world, as well as the "Pampas" of Argentine, and parts of Africa!
- Most of the serious earthquake changes will occur in the southern hemisphere.
- Europe will be physically changed quickly.
- A new people will conduct trade on seas that will cover the battlefields of WWII.
- The poles will shift between the years 2000 and 2001.
- Climates will be changed, especially cold areas becoming warmer.
- The greater portion of Japan will go into the sea.
- China will become the bedrock of Christianity (though it will be a very long time before this happens).
- Out of Russia will come the hope of the world. In stating this, Cayce implies that it will be done by some cooperative relationship with the U.S.
- Volcanic eruptions will increase in the Torrid areas around the equator.
- There will be a return to the land for mankind.
- After the earth changes, people will not build huge megalopolises like we presently have from D.C. to Boston. Rather, industries will be spread out across the countryside.
- Safety lands will be Ohio, Illinois, Indiana, Virginia,

portions of southern Canada. Of course, he indicates Montana and some portions of the Great Plains, such as Nebraska.

• The power center of the world would always be in Washington, D.C.

EDGAR CAYCE'S GREAT PYRAMID CONNECTION

As we have seen in several readings, Cayce associates many events with a time-line recorded in the Great Pyramid of Giza.

The most important number to come out of the Pyramid research of the late 1800s and the early 1900s is the pyramid inch: 365.242 pyramid inches is the geometric circle upon which the design of the Great Pyramid is based. As this number continued to appear in different areas of the structure, it was realized that this was a special measurement. It is the exact number of days in our solar year, and as such it revealed that the Great Pyramid was also a stone chronogram, recording a prophecy of coming events. Since the pyramid circle is equal to one year in Earth time, some seekers were able to measure the history of humanity, past and future.

On the following pages are diagrams by David Davidson, with time related to the inches within the Great Pyramid.

The diagrams show how the floor plan of the Great Pyramid relates to historic time. Edgar Cayce reading 5748-6 supports this concept, saying: "In those conditions that are signified in the way through the pyramid [are the] periods through which the world has passed and is passing, as related to the religious or the spiritual experiences of man." In this reading, given July 1, 1932, he said:

> The period of the present [1932] is represented by the low passage or depression show-

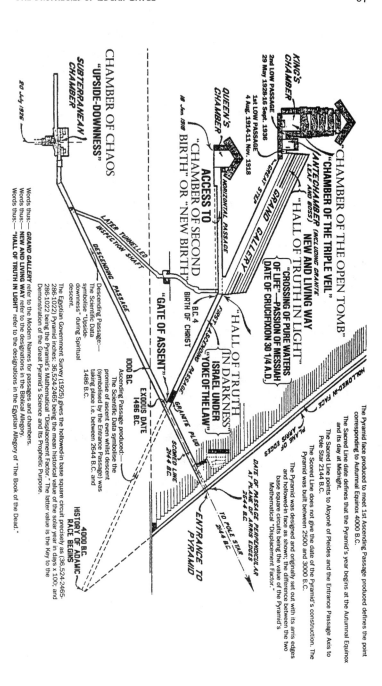

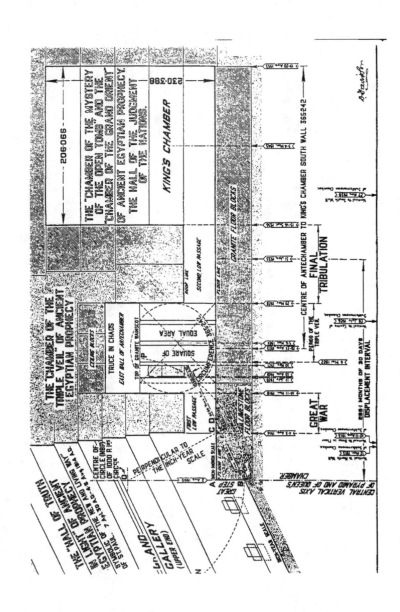

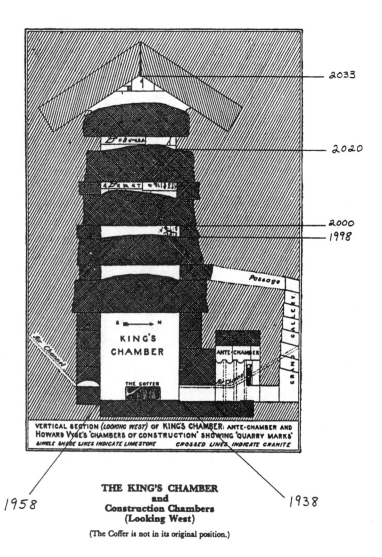

**THE KING'S CHAMBER
and
Construction Chambers
(Looking West)**

(The Coffer is not in its original position.)

ing a downward tendency, as indicated by the variations in the character of stone used. This might be termed in the present as the Cruciatarian Age [cruciat means a crusade, and often was used with the word torturing or tormenting, such as cruciatory torturing], or that in which preparations are being made *for the beginning of a new sub-race*, or a change, which—as indicated from the astronomical or numerical conditions—dates from the latter portion or middle portion of the present fall [1932]. In October, there will be a period in which the benevolent influences of Jupiter and Uranus will be stronger, which—from an astrological viewpoint—will bring a greater interest in occult or mystic influences. At the correct time, accurate imaginary lines can be drawn from the opening of the Great Pyramid to the second star in the Great Dipper, called Polaris or the North Star. This indicates it is the system toward which the soul takes its flight after having completed its sojourn through this solar system. In October, there will be seen the first variation in the position of the polar star in relation to the lines from the Great Pyramid. The dipper is gradually changing, and when this change becomes noticeable—as might be calculated from the Pyramid—there will be *the beginning of the change in the races.* There will come a greater influx of souls from the Atlantean, Lemurian, La, Ur or Da civilizations. These conditions are indicated in this turn in the journey through the Pyramid. [my italics]

How was this begun? Who was given that this should be a record of man's experiences in this root race? For that is the period covered by the prophecies in the pyramid. This was given by Ra and Hermes in that period during the reign of Araaraart when there were many who sought to bring to man a better understanding of the close relationship between the Creative Forces and that created, between man and man, and man and his Maker.

Only those who have been called may truly understand. Who then has been called? Whosoever will make himself a channel may be raised to that of a blessing. That is all that entity-body is able to comprehend. Who, having his whole measure full, would desire more does so to his own undoing

Q: What definite details are indicated as to what will happen after we enter the period of the King's Chamber?

A: When the bridegroom is at hand, all do rejoice. When we enter that understanding of being in the King's presence, with that of the mental seeking—the joy, the buoyancy, the new understanding, the new life, through the period.

Q: What is the significance of the empty sarcophagus?

A: That there will be no more death. Don't misunderstand or misinterpret! But the INTERPRETATION of death will be made plain.

Q: If the Armageddon is foretold in the Great Pyramid, please give a description of it and the date of its beginning and ending.

A: Not in what is left there. It will be as a thousand years, with the fighting in the air, and between those returning to and those leaving the earth.

Q: What is the date, as recorded by the Pyramid, of entering in the King's Chamber?
A: '38 to '58. [notice how Davidson has it as
'36 to '53] (5748-6)

Cayce goes on to say that when we reach the far wall
of the King's Chamber, then we are to proceed up the
wall, something Davidson never realized. Cayce instructs us in 5748-5 to also notice the variations in stone,
color, layers, markings and turns as we make "passage
through same, from the base to the top—to the open
tomb AND the top." All of these variations indicate
changes in "religious thought in the world." Notice how
this is measured in the third illustration. From the floor
of the King's Chamber to the top is from 1958 to approximately 2033.

When Cayce was asked in this reading "Are the deductions and conclusions arrived at by D. Davidson and H.
Aldersmith in their book on the Great Pyramid correct?"
he answered, "Many of these that have been taken as
deductions are correct. Many are far overdrawn. Only an
initiate may understand." Finally, when asked, "In which
pyramid are the records of the Christ?" he answered,
"That yet to be uncovered." (5749-2)

Key to Cayce's vision of these times is his continual
reference to a new sub-race or human body type. He
states that the pyramid chronogram actually only runs
until this new body is formed. Apparent in his readings
are a identifiable stages leading to this event. In the reading 378-14 that we have quoted from earlier, he says,
"The old record in Giza is from the journey to the
Pyrenees, to the death of the Son of Man, as a man, and
then to 1998." As we continue in this book, we will see
how the Pyrenees are also a part of the Nostradamus and
Divine Feminine material. Apparently, humanity took a
major turn in its develop as it reached that area. The

death of the Son of Man as a man, is clearly seen by Cayce as another key transition toward this new body. In or near 1998 we will take another step toward this body.

Since the last dating in the Great Pyramid is, depending on how one measures it, from 2033 to 2038 A.D., we can assume that this new sub-race will be completed in or near that date.

3

The Prophecies
of Nostradamus
(1503-1566 A.D.)

In the year 1555, Michel de Nostradame published the first edition of his prophetic book series, *Centuries*. He was already a well-known author, having published an annual almanac since 1550, and was famed for his cure for the Black Death (plague) of the Middle Ages. However famous he was in his lifetime, it does not compare to the fame he has gained since his death.

Now known throughout the world as "Nostradamus," he was born to Jewish parents in a Europe under the dark, suspicious gaze of the Inquisition. His parents raised him Roman Catholic, but converted Jews were highly suspect by the Inquisitioners. And although he was a doctor, trained at the best medical school of his time, he was not readily accepted by his peers. These were the days when medicine was dominated by the practice of blood-letting with leeches, which Nostradamus openly refused to do, choosing to treat with clean drinking water, clean bathing water, clean garments and bedding, herbs and rose hip pills of his own making, which were as popular then as our vitamin-C pills are today. When you combine his questionable religious legitimacy and his questionable medical practices with his prophesying, he was in very grave danger of the fear and suspicion of the people of his time. Nostradamus once wrote, "Here where I reside, I carry on my work among animals, barbarians, mortal enemies of learning and letters." If it were not for his success with curing plague victims and prophesying accurately for the Royal families in secular power, he probably would have died at the burning stake of the Inquisition. When you consider that he was most certainly practicing an ancient, and mostly pagan, method of divination in order to receive his visions, he was, according to the Inquisition's list of evils, a perfect example of the evil that "must be purged from our presence." Fortunately, they never quite got their hands on him. He died, as he prophesied, on July 2, 1566 in the exact position and manner that he had foreseen.

In the beginning of his *Centuries* series he describes his method as follows:

> Seated alone in secret study
> Alone it rests on the brazen tripod
> A slender flame licks out of the solitude
> Making possible that which would otherwise
>   have been vain.
>
> The wand in his hand is placed between the
>   branches

> He moistens the hem of his garment and his
>   foot
> Fear arises and a voice sets him trembling in
>   his robes
> In divine splendor, a god sits nearby.
> > —Century 1, Quatrains 1 & 2

Anyone familiar with the manuscripts *De Mysteriis Egyptorum* by Iamblichus, *De Demonibus* by Michael Psellus and the legendary *The Key of Solomon*, all forbidden by the Inquisition, would know that these two quatrains reveal a knowledge of the specific methods used in these manuscripts for the evocation of spirits. To be in possession of one of these manuscripts was enough to put you to the torture of the Inquisitioners. To be actually using the guidance in such works would send you to the stake. There is little doubt that Nostradamus was using his modified version of ancient methods for conjuring up the forces and conditions necessary for him to see the visions. The "it" in the second line of the first quatrain was either a black mirror (a black concave piece of polished metal) or a tray of specially prepared water into which he would gaze. He wrote to his son that the visions came to him in the manner of "imaginative impression" revealed by "God Almighty." Imaginative impression may be exactly what Edgar Cayce was trying to teach to his followers when he encouraged them to develop the "imaginative forces."[1]

In this next quatrain, notice how Nostradamus warns all readers, but notice also that, though he pays homage to the Christian power of his time—and there's much evidence that he genuinely was a believer in Christ—he also allows for other practitioners as long as they are "priest of the rite;" in other words, initiates into the secret teachings and methods.

> Let those who read these quatrains reflect ma-
> turely
> Let the profane, the vulgar and the common
> herd be kept away
> Let all—idiot astrologers, non-Christians—
> stay distant
> Who does otherwise, let them be priest of the
> rite.
>
> —Century 6, Quatrain 100

Since he was himself an astrologer, the third line must refer to ignorant, mundane astrologers without a clear vision of the cosmos, not all astrologers. We know that Nostradamus prayed, fasted, donned special garments and went through an elaborate preparation ceremony before beginning to gaze into the future—all the trappings of a "priest of the rite."

THE PROBLEM INTERPRETING HIS PROPHECIES

Nostradamus deliberately obscured his prophecies. His quatrains (four line poems) are not in any sequential order, making it very difficult to establish a clear timeline for the events and to get the whole picture on any particular event or series of events. One literally has to go through the nearly 1,000 quatrains and find everything that appears to refer to a singular major event, such as the Second World War, and then, putting them together, try to establish the sequence of events and people involved. In addition to the jumbled arrangement of the quatrains, he deliberately modified names and places using anagrams or ancient and foreign-language names for these people and places. So, though he wrote mostly in French, his quatrains are peppered with Latin, Greek, and several other languages. His anagrams for the names of people and places are difficult to see with foresight; much easier to see with hindsight. For example, he sees a new country coming in the distant future (he's viewing in the mid 1500s, seeing into the mid 1700s) and calls this country *l'Americh*, unmistakably America; he calls a future leader *Hister* and *Ister*, which most believe is a reference to Hitler; and the strange name *Pau Nay Loron* is likely the anagram for *Napaulon Roy* or "Napoleon the King."

In the Preface to *Centuries*, Nostradamus says that he wrote them "in dark and abstruse sayings . . . under a cloudy figure" for fear of controversy. And I would add, the dangers of a population that was so afraid of the unknown that they tended to kill it rather than try to understand it. In fact, Nostradamus was once nearly killed by a mob who were spooked by his accurate foresight into the death of their king, Henry II. This was the quatrain:

> The young lion will overcome the old one
> In single combat on a field of battle
> In a golden cage his eyes will be pierced
> Two wounds as one, followed by a cruel death
>   1:35[2]

The old lion was known in his lifetime to be King Henry II, who used the emblem of the lion (line 1). Shortly after the publication of this quatrain, King Henry II was killed during a joust (line 2) in which his opponent was a young Scottish Captain who also used the emblem of the lion. The young captain's lance splintered upon impact and a piece went through the visor of the golden helmet (cage, line 3) of the old king, piercing his eye and brain, causing him to die a slow and painful death over the next ten days (line 4). An angry mob ran through the streets of Paris looking to burn the prophet for his accuracy—the old "kill the messenger" approach to bad news. Fortunately, Henry's queen was a strong supporter of Nostradamus, so he was spared. The queen turned all attention upon the Captain's role in the death of the king, and it was the Captain that had to escape to England for fear of his life.

Still, it was considered by everyone to be a most accurate prophecy, causing Nostradamus to gain the mixed blessing of fame and suspicion of sorcery. He was right to try to obscure his prophecies so that only those who had the training and wisdom could decipher them.

I am not going to make something out of quatrains that are simply too difficult to interpret. Fortunately, there are many quatrains that are very clear in their meaning and to whom and what they refer. It is these quatrains on which we will focus our attention.

HIS PROPHECIES

I have divided the selected prophecies into four sections: (1) Those dealing with the anti-christ, since this figure is always associated with the end times; (2) Those dealing with heavenly signs, since even Jesus references the signs in the heavens as signposts of coming changes; (3) Those dealing with the sequence of Popes and their relevance to the end times; and finally, (4) Earth changes.

The Prophecies of Anti-christ

Most interpreters of Nostradamus' quatrains agree that he foresaw three great antichrists, namely: Napoleon, Hitler, and someone named "Mabus" and/or "Alus," which are most certainly anagrams or coded versions of the real name or names. Without a doubt, Napoleon and Hitler were destroyers of the world Nostradamus knew—all of Europe, England, Russia, Scandinavia and North Africa felt the sting of their war machines. Each leader fit the prophecies which stated that the anti-christ would always appear to be a god-send in the beginning of his reign, and the masses would rally behind him with great hope and expectations, only to see him turn into a demanding tyrant that would tolerate no opposition, and would send their children into bloody battles of unclear purpose until the death counts were so shocking as to numb the surviving population. Napoleon's reign resulted in over a million deaths. Hitler's reign killed millions upon millions.

Here are some of the key quatrains relating to these first two antichrists. Remember, Nostradamus is viewing Napoleon's reign some two hundred years before it occurred, and Hitler's some four hundred years! Yet, his accuracy is amazing. This again supports Edgar Cayce's teaching that everything begins in the spirit, takes shape in the mind and then ultimately manifests in the physical. Therefore, Nostradamus could see the physical events while they were still in the mental and spiritual dimensions.

Napoleon Bonaparte (1769-1821; Emperor 1804-1815)

> An Emperor will be born near Italy
> Who will cost his Empire dearly
> They will say, 'With what people he keeps company!'
> He is less of a prince than a butcher.
>
> 1:60

Napoleon was born on the island of Corsica, very near Italy (line 1). He declared himself Emperor, but he was more a war-driven soldier than prince, butchering men his greatest skill (line 4). Nostradamus reveals this ruler's non-royal claim to the throne of France and his war-driven power in the following quatrain.

> Bearing a name which no French King passed
>   on to him
> More fearsome than a thunderbolt
> Tremble will Italy, Spain and England
> Of a strange woman greatly attentive.
>
>   4:54

It is unclear who the strange woman was, perhaps Josephine, though being a traveling soldier, he had many strange women. He also had a strong relationship with his mother. Perhaps she was the attentive strange woman that Nostradamus saw in his dark mirror.

> Pau, Nay, Loron more fire than blood will be
> In praise to swim, the great man will flee to the
>   confluence.
> He will refuse entry to the pies
> And the depraved ones of France will keep
>   them confined.
>
>   8:1

The three names that begin this quatrain are towns in western France, but as we already noted, Nostradamus is playing a word game with us. If one rearranges these letters, one gets "Napaulon Roy." Napaulon is the *Corsican* spelling of Napoleon! Roy means "King." Interpreters of Nostradamus have pointed out that Napoleon was born under the fire sign, Leo, and, since he was not of the royal bloodline, he was truly "more fire than blood." J.H. Brennan points out that "pies" in line 3 "is a colloquial French diminutive of 'magpies' which, in the original, shares the same spelling as the name Pius." This links the verse immediately with two Popes, Pius VI and VII, both of whom were actually imprisoned by Napoleon in his capacity as head of what Nostradamus would certainly have considered a 'depraved' state (line 4). There is even an explanation of the curious term 'confluence' (line 2) in that Pius VI was taken by Napoleon to Valence to die on the confluence of the rivers Rhone and Isere."[3] This is even clearer in the following quatrain:

> Roman Pontiff, beware of approaching
> A city which is bathed by two rivers
> Your blood will be brought up
> You and yours when blooms the rose.
>
> 2:97

Napoleon had Pius VI and thirty-two of his priests taken to Valence, which is bathed by two rivers. There the Pope died, vomiting blood (line 3), on August 29, 1799, the summer season when roses bloom (line 4).

In the following quatrain we have a clear description of this antichrist:

> To the Great Empire [France] quite a different
>   man comes
> Being distant from kindness and happiness
> Ruled by one not long from his bed
> While the kingdom to great unhappiness.
>
> 6:67

History has described Napoleon as a "brooding, lonely, unhappy man (line 2), sometimes strongly influenced by the women who came to his bed (line 3, notably Josephine)."[4] But all the while, the great kingdom of France moves ever closer to disaster and unhappiness (line 4).

The end of Napoleon's reign was seen by Nostradamus this way:

The part of Rome ruled by he who interprets
   the Augur [i.e., the Pope]
By the French will be much vexed
But the French nation will rue the hour
of the North Wind [Russia] and the fleet [Eng-
   land] when they drive too far.

                              2:99

Napoleon drove France and her young men too far,
gaining the wrath of Rome, the deadly winter of Russia
and the English fleet with her armies. Ultimately, France
was defeated and rued the hour that they began following this antichrist. But history repeats in rhythms and
cycles. Europe gives life to another great anti-christ.

Adolf Hitler (1889-1945)

In the following quatrains we read Nostradamus' visions of the coming of another anti-christ who would
ravage Europe and beyond, leaving a trail of blood, brutality, and betrayal. He will begin as all anti-christs, by
seducing the populus with what they want to hear. Then,
he will make them pay dearly for their support.

From the depth of Western Europe
From poor people a child will be born
Who with his tongue will seduce a great crowd
   of people
His fame increases in the Eastern Kingdom.

                              3:35

Hitler was born in Austria, the depths of Western Europe (line 1), to poor parents (line 2). His speeches
mesmerized the crowds (line 3). And, his reputation increased his relationship with Japan (the Eastern Kingdom of line 4), resulting in the signing of the Tripartite
Pact between Germany, Italy and Japan.

Liberty will not be recovered
It will be occupied by a black, fierce and
    wicked villian;
When the question of the Pontiff is raised
By D'Hister [Hitler], the Italian republic will be
    angry.

5:29

Once allowed a foothold, Hitler and Nazism never stopped their advance, taking liberty and occupying people's lives and lands with a black, fierce wickedness (lines 1 & 2). Also, the Schutzstaffel, or SS, wore black uniforms and were the elite guard and exterminators for Hitler (line 2). And when the question of the Pope was presented to Hitler, he responded "I will go right into the Vatican!" (line 3) And, of course, under Mussolini and the Tripartite Pact, Hitler and Mussolini angered many free-dom-loving people, including many Italians. (line 4)

Beasts, driven insane with hunger, will cross
    the rivers
The greater part of the field will go to Ister
    [Hitler]
In a cage of iron the great will be dragged away
When the child of Germany observes nothing.

2:24

Hitler's armies and their methods and the subsequent governors that ruled in the wake of their victories were like beasts, driven insane with a hunger to possess and purge the world (line 1). In railroad boxcars, many of Europe's great leaders and peoples were dragged away (line 3) by this child of Germany who observed no laws, borders, or any forms of human decency; nothing (line 4)!

In a spot not too far removed from Venice
The two strongest of Asia [Japan] and Africa
[Italy]
Will be said to come together with the Rhine
[Germany] and Ister [Hitler]
Weeping at Malta and the Ligurian coast.—
4:68

The Tripartite Axis Pact was signed between Germany, Italy and Japan at the Brenner Pass, not too far from Venice (line 1). Italy annexed Ethiopia, making it the strongest power in Africa (line 2). Malta and Genoa (the Ligurian coast) were both bombarded heavily during the war; Malta by the Axis powers and Genoa by the Allies (line 4).

As Nostradamus prophesied, just as the French would rue the hour they brought Napoleon to power, so the Germans would pity the day they brought Hitler to power. But, it is the bane of humanity that they forget, and so a third anti-christ will rise up, more terrible than the two that preceded him.

Mabus and/or Alus

Since this name belongs to one yet to be seen, it is more difficult to identify and interpret the quatrains related to him/her, except where Nostradamus clearly uses the name Mabus and Alus, or refers to the anti-christ in a context not fitting Napoleon or Hitler. Erika Cheetham suggests that Mabus and Alus may be "corruptions" of the Latin word "Malus," which means "Evil One." Nostradamus only mentions these two names once in separate quatrains. Here they are:

Mabus will come, and soon after will die
Of people and beasts a great destruction
Suddenly, vengeance will be seen

Blood, hand, thirst, famine, when the comet
   passes.

2:62

His last hand through bloody Alus
Will not save him by sea
Between two rivers he will fear the military
   hand
The black and wrathful one makes repentant.

6:33

These quatrains do appear to be very specific. We can
see in them that the anti-christ is bloody, destructive,
vengeful, and brings famine and thirst. We can also see
that a comet passing is a sign of his presence. Somehow,
hands play a key role in his activities (line 4 in the first
quatrain and lines 1 and 3 in the second). Erika Cheetham has proposed that the "military hand" may be the
nuclear "finger on the button" of the 1950s through the
1990s. In line 3 the complete annihilation of humanity
(which began between the two rivers of the Tigris and
Euphrates in the Garden of Eden, where Satan first
gained influence) causes even the Evil One to fear the
loss of everything, leaving nothing for him to rule. Line
4, "The black and wrathful one makes repentant," is a
curious statement. Nostradamus uses the French word
"noir" here, which most interpreters translate as "black."
But noir also means dark. Perhaps this is a reference to
the coming day of the Lord, when the sun will not give
its light. Noir also has a connotation of "evil." Perhaps it
is a reference to the forces of evil and Satan in the context that St. Paul uses in 1 Cor. 5:5, "Hand this man over
to Satan, so that the sinful nature may be destroyed and
his spirit saved on the day of the Lord." The Lord's day is
marked by his wrath on all evil—causing many to repent
from their support of the antichrist influence.

The 1900s have been filled with wars. Some of them the likes of which the world has never seen, with more bloodshed than any other period—millions upon millions butchered. Few nations on the earth have avoided some confrontation and bloodshed during this period. As for the passing comet in the Mabus quatrain, it would certainly appear to be Nostradamus' way of dating the coming of this antichrist, but there are many comets, and many have come and gone when the world seemed in great peril.

A Date for the Antichrist

We may have the clearest dating of the coming of the antichrist (and/or a reference to the two beasts of the Revelation) in these next quatrains.

> In the year 1999 and seven months [July]
> From the sky will come a great King of Terror
> To resuscitate the great King of the Mongols
> Before and after, Mars reigns happily
>
> 10:72

Certainly this is one of the clearest datings in the whole of Nostradamus' work. It would appear to fit with the prophecies of the Armageddon, a battle fought in the "air" (line 2, "from the sky") between the forces of good and evil.

The resuscitating of the King of the Mongols (line 3) is a terrible thought. History still holds the Mongol Hordes and their reign throughout all of Asia and much of Europe during the 1200s as one of the most brutal, cruel, barbarious periods ever. India, Persia, Russia, and Eastern Europe all suffered the murderous brutality of these conquerors. When the Mongols defeated the armies of Western Europe, the Vatican and the Holy Land were open to invasion without resistance, and all Christendom appeared to be lost. Then, a miracle happened; the great Khan died! To everyone's shock, the Mongol hordes returned home to morn and fight among themselves, leaving much of the West to rebuild itself.

If we are to assume from this quatrain that these cruel souls are to rise again from the dead to spread their uncaring brutality across the planet, then this is the worst of predictions, suited well to Jesus' statement that lawlessness will reign so freely that the hearts of many will grow cold.[5] However, Nostradamus does not clearly say they will assault the world; perhaps a more local event along the lines of China's brutal invasion of Tibet would be enough to fulfill this prophecy. If the date is right, then we will certainly find out on or shortly after July 1999.

The Cayce readings support this prophecy, saying that if the world does not get its act together, then "a hated people will be raised up" among the yellow race. This could be Nostradamus' "resuscitation of the great King of the Mongols."

Nostradamus also foresees the rising of a leader who declares Thursday as his holy day. Islam has Friday, Judaism Saturday, and Christianity Sunday; but this new leader will apparently reform some current religion or develop a new one with Thursday as the holy day. It is not clear if this person is an anti-christ or a good leader, but there are some hints:

> From the aquatic triplicity will be born
> One who will have Thursday for his holy day
> His fame, praise, rule and power will grow
> By land and sea to become a tempest to the
> Orient.
>
> 1:50

"From the aquatic triplicity" could mean the three water signs of the zodiac: Cancer, Scorpio and Pisces.

Perhaps these will be predominant in his horoscope. Or, as Henry Roberts suggests,[6] perhaps the aquatic triplicity is the Atlantic, Pacific and Gulf of Mexico; in other words, the U.S.A. with Thanksgiving as its special day, the last *Thursday* of November. Certainly the U.S. has been giving the Orient (line 4) much attention (China in the early 1900s, Japan in the 40s, Korea in the 50s, Vietnam in the 60s and 70s, Taiwan and again China in the 80s, and again China and North Korea in the 90s). The U.S. has had many ongoing interactions with the Orient, good and bad, by land and sea (line 4). In this case then the man in the quatrain could be Franklin D. Roosevelt who officially declared Thanksgiving *Thursday* as a U.S. national holiday. This is supported by another quatrain that does appear to foreshadow the founding of the new, "fair" land to which many will come and give honor, namely America. This new country begins in the freezing cold winters of Plymouth, Massachusetts but leads to a Thursday of Thanksgiving.

> The land and air will freeze with so much water
> When they come to venerate Thursday
> That which will be, never was so fair
> Of the four quarters they will come to honor him
>
> 10:71

If this is what these quatrains are referring to, then Nostradamus' visions, seen in the mid 1500s, are truly amazing. Nevertheless, I'd keep my eye open for someone else declaring Thursday as his holy day. Surprisingly, we have another holy day to watch for:

> The penultimate one of the surname of the Prophet

Will take Monday for his day of rest
Wandering far because of his frenzied head
Delivering a great people from impositions.

2:28

Penultimate means "next to last," and a surname is a
name held by all members of a family. "The Prophet" is
usually a reference to Mohammed, but I don't see how
this leads to any conclusions. Perhaps Nostradamus is
referring to the prophet who saw the Revelation, St. John,
and, as we know, the Cayce readings give this prophet a
surname, Peniel. This prophet may return, make Monday his day of rest because he works weekends. It's difficult to know exactly what Nostradamus meant. The least
we can say is that Nostradamus saw two leaders using
Monday and Thursday, respectfully, as their rest day and
holy day. All we can do is wait and see how this plays out
on the world stage.

There are only two quatrains where the term "anti-
christ" is used plainly.

By the antichrist, three will be quickly annihi-
lated
Twenty-seven years of blood will last his war
The heretics dead, captive, exiled
Bloody human corpses, water red, covering
the earth.

8:77

The chief of London by l'Americh [American] power
The isle of Scotland burdened with ice [frost?]
Roy Reb will have so dreadful an antichrist
Who will put them all in discord.

10:66

Could the "three" (line 1) of the first quatrain be the

same as the three in the second quatrain, namely, London, America and Scotland? Or is Scotland only used as a sign that a major climate change has occurred, putting Scotland under ice and an island separated from the English mainland (line 2)?

Who or what is Roy Reb? Roy means "king," but Reb is unclear. In Judaism, Reb is a form of Rabbi. Perhaps Nostradamus is speaking of a great deceiver that leads the Jews astray or in discord with one another. However, I don't see how this relates to the first two lines of this quatrain. Of course, the 27-year-long war in the first quatrain could easily relate to the Jews, because they've been in a virtual war since the sixties; and if Nostradamus considers the Islamic opponents to be "heretics" to the teachings of Father Abraham, then his lines about "The heretics dead, captive, exiled (one of Israel's common punishments)/Bloody human corpses, water red (Red Sea?), covering the earth" has relevance to this Middle Eastern battle that has been raging for so long, and involving the whole earth in its problems.

Some interpreters say it's Rob Roy of Scotland (1671-1734), a Robin Hood character who rustled cattle and sold his neighbors protection. I don't see how that relates to these quatrains. Erika Cheetham believes the second quatrain relates to U.S. nuclear weapons being housed on Scottish soil with the permission of the chief of London, which caused much discomfort for these three governments, mostly from their own people. Actually, I'm inclined to take a broader interpretation of these two quatrains.

The antichrist is, as Edgar Cayce stated earlier, a spirit, an attitude with chillingly violent, uncaring, unthinking emotions that insidiously creeps into the hearts and minds of individuals, families, communities, nations, and leaders, blocking out the light of Christ (which is the love of God and neighbor) and bringing on the conditions necessary for "bloody human corpses, red water and discord" everywhere. Could the "three quickly annihilated" by the antichrist be "faith, hope and charity?" Could Roy Reb be just that, King Reb or Rebel—that spirit that separates oneself from a sense of oneness with others and God, allowing us to do whatever seems good to us, with complete disregard for what others might want or need, or what the Christ spirit wants? Jesus says the end times will cause hearts to grow cold; even the elect would fall away if the end time were not shortened. If we consider that Nostradamus used anagrams and word-plays, could the terms *Mabus* and *Alus* simply be:

"May-b-us" and "All us"

Is it possible that the anti-christ, no matter who personifies this spirit as a leader, requires us to give it fuel, to give it life in our hearts and minds? Notice in this quatrain how American power makes it happen. America is where the governing influence is by the people, for the people. If that influence becomes tainted with mean-spiritedness, spitefulness, revenge, intolerance, etc., then the anti-christ has gained power. The power is with the people, each of us, in our hearts and minds. We then give power to families, communities, nations and leaders. What spirit will rule? As God said in Genesis, Evil's "desire is for you, but you must master it." Or, "Go. Be fruitful and multiply, but *subdue* the earth" and its influence upon you.

May be us, all of us, have to take hold of our free wills and responsibility for our thoughts and actions, and hold others to a high responsibility for their actions and thoughts.

The Prophecies of Heavenly Signs
Just as all the End-Times prophets have written,

Nostradamus also writes that there will be signs in the heavens.

> The great star for seven days will burn
> A cloud will make two suns appear
> The big mastiff will howl all night
> When a great Pope changes his territory.
>
> 2:41

I am sitting here writing this chapter on July 18, 1994, the week that Jupiter, a planet composed of the same gases as our Sun, only much cooler, is being bombarded with 21 comet fragments the size of mountains, causing great clouds of debris to rise from the surface of this huge planet. The comet bombardment will last six days, but perhaps the planet will burn for one more day, matching Nostradamus' seven-day prediction (line 1). By the time this book is published, you will already know whether this cosmic event was the one Nostradamus was viewing in his vision.

The two-suns prophecy is also among the Mother-Mary prophecies, but it does not appear in any of the scriptural or Cayce prophecies, unless the phrase, "His star [sometimes, "His light"] will be seen in the heavens" is referring to another star or sun appearing in our system. Of course, many interpreters of Nostradamus consider this to be a comet rather than a star or sun. This is probably because it is much easier to conceive of a comet than another sun in our system! But the prophet wrote, "two suns." However, he did say that the cloud makes it *appear* as though there are two suns. So, perhaps it's an illusion rather than a reality.

The mastiff howling all night is an ominous sign of danger and death since the mastiff is a watch dog. As we shall see in the next section, changes in the Papacy are useful signs for timing these quatrains. If the Pope moves his abode or even leaves this world (line 4) during or soon after the star burns for 7 days, I'd be prepared for the Mastiff to howl.

There are quatrains that appear to refer to comets. One of them we have already discussed. It began with the reference to Mabus and ended with this line: "Blood, hand, thirst, famine, when the comet passes." [2:62] In another quatrain, Nostradamus refers to a "bearded star;" presumably, he means a *comet* [2:15]. "In the sky will be seen a fire with a tail of sparks" [2:46] also seems to be describing a comet.

The world has seen some major comets since the time of Nostradamus: Nexel in 1720, Kohoutek in 1974, IRAS-Araki-Alcock in 1983 (the closest known comet in the past 200 years), Halley's in 1986 and now the great comet bombardment of Jupiter in 1994. To Nostradamus and most other religious seekers of the Middle Ages, a comet was always a bad omen, a sign of coming disaster. Actually, any heavenly phenomenon is a bad omen because, to them, it portends of "the great and terrible day of the coming of the Lord!" I suppose the star of Bethleham is one famous example of a heavenly sign of the coming of the Lord. And, if you were among the mothers of newborn boy-babies in Bethlehem, then the star was a very bad omen as Herod's murdering soldiers descended upon the little town. A great Savior had been born to lead the world out of darkness, but the earth suffered much from His coming. Judas thought Jesus would lead an army against Rome, but in A.D. 70, Titus' legions destroyed the great Temple in Jerusalem, the Jews were scattered, and the Christians fed to beasts in the arena and burned at the stake. There has always been a great conflict between good and evil, light and darkness, since Michael and Lucifer first battled for control of heaven. History has recorded well that a major movement on the part of one always brings a major counter movement by the other. Jesus receives the Holy Spirit during his baptism with John, but then is led off into the desert to wrestle with Satan. A much-quoted Cayce reading says that wherever you have a channel of Light, darkness seeks to enter. Therefore, a heavenly sign is often a discomforting omen, even if it does ultimately mean a new era of greater light, greater good.

Since the current Jupiter situation includes a comet, which has become 21 comet fragments—or "tails of sparks"—and has the potential for creating a new sun (by the ignited Jupiter perhaps), it seems to be the most significant comet in the 1900s.

There are also several quatrains dealing with fire in or from the sky:

> Forty-five degrees the sky will be alight
> Fire approaches the great new city
> At once a great flame springs up
> When they wish to see the Normans proven
>
> 6:97

This last line could be the time indicator. Therefore, we might consider this quatrain to refer to the D-Day invasion at Normandy or a major anniversary celebrating that day ("to see the Normans proven"). It could also be the French people as a whole. Some interpreters believe the forty-five degrees relates to a city along the 45th parallel. As I spin the globe before me, assuming that the poles are still relatively close to our present situation, the cities that lie on or near the 45th parallel are: Portland, Minneapolis, Ottawa, Montreal, Lyon, Milan, Belgrade, and Bucharest.

To Nostradamus, viewing this scene in the 1500s, heavy guns (from ships, tanks and artillery) may appear to be firing at 45° angles from the ground, with great fires and explosions resulting. But, just to show how terribly difficult it is to understand these quatrains with foresight only, it could refer to fires on the hills surrounding the great new city of San Francisco/Oakland (a mountainside roughly a 45° angle from the flat land); or perhaps the fires around the great new city of Los Angeles, nearer the timing of the 50th anniversary of D-Day? Certainly, San Francisco and Los Angeles are very new cities, especially LA. Of course, many believe that this is speaking about a city with the word "new" in its name, i.e., New York.

Brennan believes this quatrain relates to France, a great new city in the land of the Normans, whose old capital was Rouen on the Seine River. The great new city could then be Paris on the Seine, but Paris is a bit above the 45th parallel, as is Rouen. Perhaps the world is waiting to see the French prove themselves in Bosnia through which runs the 45th parallel? Then, the new city would be Sarajevo (but it's not really new). Or, perhaps it refers to Montreal, a truly new city with French qualities. It is difficult to know until it happens, then everyone looks back in hindsight with amazement.

> By fire from the sky the city is almost razed
> Flooding again threatens Deucalion
> Sardinia vexed by the African fleet
> After Libra leaves Leo
>
> 2:81

Fire from the sky falls upon another unnamed city. This is also a difficult quatrain to interpret. In Greek mythology, Deucalion was the only human left after the great flood (a Noah-like character). According to this quatrain, even he will be in danger of not surviving the next one! Sardinia is an island country to the south of Italy in the Mediterranean Sea. A Cayce reading refers to Libya as being an earthly reflection of Libra![7] Could

Nostradamus be using this, and the African fleet is Libya's, or is it the U.S. fleet off the coast of Libya? Or, perhaps it is in a future so different from what we presently know that we can't interpret this quatrain without our own vision.

Among the heavenly signs that Nostradamus sees is a "dart of heaven," which we could naturally presume to be a comet or missile.

> The dart of heaven will make its journey
> Death spoken of, great execution
> The stone in the tree, the proud nation brought
> down
> Rumor of a human monster, purge and atone-
> ment
>
> 2:70

J.H. Brennan believes this quatrain fits the Gulf War of Desert Storm rather well. The human monster is Saddam Hussein, whose danger to us and the Middle East was fed mostly by rumors (line 4). Saddam spoke at great length about the magnitude of death (line 2) that would occur if the U.S. and its Allies attacked, referring to the conflict as the "Mother of All Battles!" But, alas, the execution was great (line 2) by the Allies, with their "darts from heaven," and a proud nation, Iraq, was brought down (line 3). I'd also like to point out that this is a nation between the two great rivers of the origin of humanity, the Tigris and Euphrates of the Garden of Eden. Could this be what is meant by "the stone in the tree" which needs purging and atonement for its sins (line 3)? The tree being The Tree of Life, from which we have been banished, and the stone being the tablets of the Ten Commandments through which we will atone and thereby regain the Tree of Life?

Of all Nostradamus' heavenly signs, the clearest are

the two suns [2:41] and the Mabus quatrain noting the passing comet as a sign [2:62]. Both of these are omens of bad times, vengeance, death, howling and a Pope changing his territory.

The Prophecies of Popes

Nostradamus' references to Popes is important because it may help us identify the timing of certain events. He seems to be aware of, or his visions give support to, the Irish bishop/prophet, Malachy, who also foresaw history via a line of specifically identified Popes.

In 1138, Malachy visited the Vatican. While there, he fell into a deep trance during which he saw the reigning pontiff and the line of succession of 112 Popes, followed by the final fall of the Church of Rome. When he awoke, he wrote a complete manuscript on the vision, giving each Pope a Latin motto. The manuscript was sent to the Vatican after Malachy's passing, where it was stored in secret archives until 1590, long after Nostradamus' death (b. 1503, d. 1566). Later, around 1730-40, a monk called "The Monk of Padua" wrote a manuscript listing a sequence of Popes and the ultimate end of the Papacy which closely followed Malachy's, also using Malachy's mottos for the Popes.

In the 20th century, Malachy calls Benedict XV, "Religio Depopulata," which could relate to his being the Pope during WWI, certainly a period of "depopulation of religion." Pius XII, 1939 to 1958, Malachy called "Pastor Angelicus," referring to his angelic shepherding of the Church. Many followers considered him extremely "saintly." He was followed by John XXIII, 1958-63, called "Pastor et Nauta" (shepherd and navigator), perhaps referring to his position as Archbishop of Venice or his reconvening of the Ecumenical Council for the first time since 1869. The Council used the symbols of a cross and a ship, perhaps indicative of the Shepherd and Navigator. After him came, "Flos Florum" (Flower of Flowers), Paul VI (1963-78). His coat of arms contained a floral design. After him came "De Mediatate Lunae" (the middle or half of the moon), John Paul I (August 26 to September 28, 1978). This is one of the shortest and most suspicious papal reigns. John Paul I was only 66 and in good health when he suddenly died. He had disturbed his Curia (Senate of Cardinals) by stating in one of his earliest speeches that God was not only the Heavenly Father but also the Heavenly Mother. He began to openly support women's rights and agreed to meet with a U.S. Congressional delegation to discuss artificial birth control! Just prior to his curious death, he asked his Secretary of State, Cardinal Jean Villot, to begin an investigation of the Vatican Bank and secret memberships of his priests in the Freemason's Lodge P2. The next morning he was dead. Investigators were surprised that Cardinal Villot initially gave them false information during their questioning and that the Cardinals quickly embalmed the body, then cremated it, against strict Catholic custom at that time. Stranger still, Cardinal Villot died within six months of these events.[8] Here's what Nostradamus wrote four hundred years ago:

> When the sepulchre of the great Roman is found
> The day after will be elected a Pope
> By his Senate he will not be approved
> Poisoned is his blood by the sacred chalice.
> 3:65

> He who will have government of the Great Cape [the Pope]
> Will be led to take action
> The twelve Red Ones [Cardinals] will come to spoil the cover

Under murder, murder will come to be done.
>   4:11

If this is ever found to be the case, the scandal will rock the Papacy to its foundations, perhaps changing it forever. Could Nostradamus be referring to this in the next quatrain:

> In the sacred temples, there will be made scan-
>   dals
> They will be thought of as honors and praise-
>   worthy matters
> By one who they mark for silver, gold and coins
> The end will be torments very strange.
>   9:6

If banking, murder and Mafia connection scandals do surface in the Vatican, it could be said that Daniel's "abomination of desolation standing where it ought not to be" may be coming true before our eyes. These types of scandals in all religions and denominations are being seen more and more, causing Daniel's abomination of desolation to come to life in a place where it ought not to be. We've seen leaders of massive congregations go down in flaming scandals of moral and financial corruption. Perhaps there will come a day when the sacred temples will be desolate of true spiritual and moral light.

After John Paul I, comes "De Labore Solis" (the labor of the sun), John Paul II, Karol Wojtyla from Poland. J.H. Brennan points out that the part of Poland from which John Paul II came was originally a portion of ancient France, and therefore the following quatrain may refer to him:

> Not from Spain, but from ancient France
> He will be elected from the trembling ship

To the enemy he will make assurance
Who in his reign will be a cruel blight

5:49

Brennan considers the trembling ship to be the Church itself. The great enemy of Polish John Paul II would be none other than the Soviet Union. John Paul II made assurances (line 3) to the Soviets concerning the strikes in Poland by the workers, assurances that may have kept them from doing what they did in Hungary and Czechoslovakia. It is said that John Paul II sent a message to Moscow that if they mounted an invasion against Poland, he would fly to Warsaw and stand, in full papal regalia, before the approaching tanks. Brennan goes on to say that though John Paul II was successful in this situation, the Soviet blight (line 4) continued through much of his early years as Pope. Then came the assassination attempt, the first one. But the second, which received little press, caught more of Nostradamus' attention:

Oh great Rome, your ruin comes close
Not of your walls, but of your blood and substance
The sharp one of letters will be so horrible a notch
Pointed steel placed up his sleeve, ready to wound.

10:65

Mehmet Ali Agca was the Turk who shot John Paul II. It was believed that the KGB was behind the shooting. But the stabber was an educated priest who, during a Papal visit to Portugal in 1982, pulled a long knife from out of his sleeve and attempted to kill John Paul II. This attempt did not receive much press. But Nostradamus certainly seems to be viewing this event, noting perhaps the failure, "your ruin comes close."

After John Paul II, the current Pope, Malachy and the Priest of Padua predict only two more: "Gloria Olivae" (glory of the olive), whom the Priest of Padua says will take the name Leo XIV, and "Petrus Romanus" (Peter of Rome). Malachy predicts that Peter of Rome will be the last Pope, and that the city will be burned. The Priest of Padua also predicts the burning of the city when the last Pope sits on the throne. When then is the end? If the present Pope continues for another few years, then give Gloria Olivae about 10 years, Peter of Rome would very likely take the throne in the early years of the 2000s.

> The great star for seven days will burn
> A cloud will make two suns appear
> The big mastiff will howl all night
> *When a great Pope changes his territory.*
>
> 2:41

It may be by war or scandal that the Pope has to change his territory. Whatever the cause, when we see a Pope changing his territory, I'd look for this quatrain's dark omen to begin.

Prophecies of Earth Changes

Are the prophecies of war and bloodshed, disease and pestilence, famine, drought, flood, and earthquake, prophecies about this century? Here are two quatrains that make one think so:

> After the great human misery, an even greater approaches
> *The great motor of the cycles [or centuries] renews [the year 2000?]*
> Rain, blood, milk, famine, sword and pestilence
> In the sky will be seen a fire with a tail of sparks.
>
> 2:46 [my italics]

Saturn and a water sign in Sagittarius
In its highest increase of exaltation
Pestilence, famine, death from military hand
*The century approaches its renewal. [the year
    2000?]*
                                        1:16 [my italics]

The first quatrain seems to be referring to the renewal
of cycles of the centuries, or a millenium, when the centuries start over. The second one is clearly referring to
the millennium. Since he was prophesing in the 1500s,
we can assume he wasn't referring back to 999 A.D.;
therefore, it is likely he is referring to 2000 A.D. However,
I want to share with you that in a letter to his son,
Nostradamus clearly says that his prophecies are from
"his time to the year 3797 A.D." Therefore, his end-times
prophecies could even relate to 3000 A.D.. Being finite
persons, we tend to see our age as *the* age.

The millennium hysteria caused near panic in 999
A.D. Christendom holds closely to the belief that the end
of the world will be at the end of a thousand-year period,
a millennium, so each millennium is met with high anxi-
ety and expectations. Naturally, those of us approaching
2000 A.D. believe it may be in our lives, as will those who
approach 3000 A.D. However, the scriptural prophecies
state that the "end times" will be followed by a one-thou-
sand year period of peace, when the Messiah will reign
and Satan will be bound.[9] Therefore, Nostradamus' 3797
could include the final 1,000 years of peace, bringing us
back to a period from 1797 through 2797 for the thousand year battle of Armegeddon (Cayce states that the
battle will last for a thousand years[10]), which ends with
the reign of the Messiah for another 1,000 years. This
would put 2000 A.D. as a major but not a climactic
millenium mark. Significant changes may well occur,
physically and spiritually, but the passing of earth and

heaven, as Jesus spoke of it,[11] is not yet.

As with all the end times and earth changes prophecies, earthquakes and floods top the list of predicted events; great fires appear, the loss of major cities, and a pole shift, though this isn't as clear in Nostradamus' writings as it is in Cayce's. Here are some of the quatrains that appear to predict earth changes:

> Near Auch, Lectoure and Mirande
> A great fire will fall from the sky for three nights
> A thing will happen stupendous and miraculous
> And shortly after the ground will tremble.
>
> 1:46

Some interpreters believe this quatrain refers to a comet falling to earth followed by earthquakes. Others believe it refers to our first true visitation by aliens in ships that appear as fires in the night, their landing causing the whole ground to shake. The thing that strikes me from this quatrain is the mention of the city of Auch, the capital of ancient Gascony, which included the Pyrenees Mountains. The Cayce readings clearly identify a major cycle beginning in ancient Egypt and continuing to the Pyrenees Mountains, then on to the year 1998. Cayce's teaching that a new body will appear, referencing St. Paul's comment about us all being changed,[12] could be the "thing will happen stupendous and miraculous" (line 3).

> They will think to have seen the sun at night
> When the pig, half a man is seen
> Noise, chants, battles which appear fought in the sky
> And brute beasts will be heard to speak.
>
> 1:64

This is a strange one. It seems to be about an extremely bright light at night, with battles fought in the sky and a pig that is half man, with animals speaking. Animals speaking could be Nostradamus' viewing of our work with dolphins, chimpanzees, and selected birds. The pig that is half man is seen by Erika Cheetham as a modern-day jet pilot in his oxygen mask, helmet, goggles and flight suit, fighting a battle in the air—which Nostradamus would have seen as very strange. In fact, a battle of this nature may also appear as bright as daylight though it was being fought at night. Jets and bombs make tremendous noise and strange sounds; perhaps rockets and missiles sound like droning chants until they strike (line 3). Ms. Cheetham could be right about this one. If so, it is only a view into our times by a 16th century man, having nothing to do with earth changes per se.

> The great famine which I see approaching
> Turning one way and then another, then be-
>   coming universal
> So great and long that they will pluck
> The roots from the wood and the child from
>   the breast.
>
> 1:67

Has the world already seen much of this famine? Is it the worldwide Great Depression of the 1930s? Or, is it still winding its way across the planet, ultimately coming to all nations and lands? The last line of this quatrain is reminiscent of Jesus saying "woe to those who nurse babies" during the end times.[13] As I view the African famines on television, those nursing mothers seem sorrowfully helpless, their bodies unable to produce even the basic nourishment for their babies.

> Ennosigee [Earth-shaking] fire from the cen-
>   ter of the earth
> Will make trembling all around the New City
> Two great rocks will long war against each
>   other
> Then, Arethusa will color red the new river.
>
> 1:87

Two great rocks warring against each other would be an excellent description of tectonic plates, just as we see in the Western portion of America, particularly California, and in Japan. Since Nostradamus precedes this tectonic war with "fire from the center of the earth," I'm inclined to look for volcanic activity to precede the quake and the trembling of the New City. In his time, Paris, London and Rome were great cities, so it must be one of the newer cities on a tectonic plate, perhaps Los Angeles, San Francisco, San Diego, Tokyo (which would be a new city for Nostradamus) or even New York, though New York's fault has not been warring a long time and L.A.'s has. This quatrain seems to fit California's cities better than any others.

The name "Arethusa" (line 4) is from Greek mythology. Arethusa was a woodland nymph and one of the attendants of Artemis (goddess of the moon, Apollo's twin sister). Alpheus, a river god, saw her bathing in a stream and tried to embrace her. As she fled under the sea, she called on Artemis for help and was changed into a fountain. It was believed that Alpheus, in the form of a river, flowed underground to Sicily, where he was united with her in the fountain of Arethusa in the city of Syracuse. There is also an orchid/herb called "Dragon's-mouth," its botanical name *Arethusa bulbosa*. Known also as "swamp pink," it grows in swamps and bogs from Newfoundland south to North Carolina, and west to Minnesota. Could the "new river" that Arethusa colors red be in these areas? If it is the Midwest of the U.S., then this could be the same prophecy as Cayce's — the Great Lakes will empty into the Gulf of Mexico, turning the Mississippi red with blood of victims? Then, the "new city" on the 45th parallel could be from Minneapolis to Montreal. The Dragon's mouth may well be a reference to increased volcanic activity which precedes the new river's movement. Again, it's difficult to know.

Critics of Nostradamus' work say that almost anything can be predicted using his quatrains because they are so open to interpretation. I've tried to select those that have some specificity to them. Certainly, his specific dating of July 1999 cannot be open to interpretation.

I'll close this chapter with one more of his quatrains:

> Twenty years of the moon's reign pass
> Seven thousand years another monarch shall
>   hold
> When the sun takes up his days
> Then shall my prophecies be complete
>
> 1:48

Seven thousand years is a long time. I believe we have many more adventures to enjoy and make the most of before the real end comes. What we are approaching now is a great change from one era to another. It will be challenging and transforming.

4

The Messages from the Holy Mother
(The Divine Feminine)

There have been hundreds of reported appearances of the Holy Mother. "Apparition" has become the word used to describe these visions, a word that means "to unexpectedly appear, to become visible without warning or preparation." It also refers to "a phantom or ghost." Everyone that has reported seeing the image agrees that it is *not* physical, is surrounded by light, sound, and movement that is not normal, and appears without warning or invitation. The seers are usually engaged in everyday activities when suddenly she appears. Her appearance is sometimes accompanied by lightning or a clap of thunder. In some cases, she is preceded by the appearance of a male "light-being," or angel. Sometimes the angel has identified himself as the archangel Michael, whom we know as the archangel of the heavenly battle against Lucifer. The Female-image identifies herself in different ways, calling herself at different times: The Lady of Peace, The Queen of Peace, The Immaculate Heart; to the children in Rwanda, Africa she called herself "The Mother of the World," which appears to be a clear reference to Genesis' name for Eve, "The Mother of All."

There are some consistent features to these apparitions. She is always bright with light, a veil over her head, wearing a seamless dress (often white, once blue), barefoot, and able to move without walking—most describe her movement as "gliding." She is always suspended above the ground, and appears and disappears with great speed. As mentioned earlier, her appearance is usually accompanied by lightning and/or thunder, or some unusual sound with light. Colors frequently associated with her appearances are starlight white and sky blue.

Her appearance and language have a universal quality to them. The black children to whom she appeared in Africa could not recall what "color" her skin was. They described her as being "like them," but not black, white or "half caste." To the white girls in Medjugorje, Yugoslavia, her skin color was not discernible, except that she was not white like her pictures, but neither was she any other color. She spoke in the native language of each group that saw her (Tolpetlac, Spanish, French, Portuguese, Slavic, Rwandan, English, and so on).

Overall, her teachings are universal in their tone and content, supporting no specific faith or doctrine. For example, to the children in Medjugorje she said, "There is only one God and one Faith." To the children in Rwanda she said, "Before God there is neither Protestant nor Catholic, nor Adventist, nor Moslem, nor any branch of other creeds. The true son of God is whoever does God's will." A Catholic priest in the Rwandan school where the apparitions occurred notes that "the Lady" never asked the Protestant or Moslem pupils to "become Catholic, but to recognize her as the Mother of God."

A peculiar and fascinating fact about these apparitions is the progression of the time of day that she appeared—beginning before dawn in the Guadalupe apparition in 1531, morning in Lourdes in 1858, noon in Fatima in 1917, evening in Medjugorje in 1981 and the nightfall appearances later that same year in Rwanda. This progression fits well with ancient mystical teachings that the progression of the Sun through the heavens reflects the progression of humanity through the earth.

The earliest I could find of her apparitions was 1251 A.D., when she appeared to Simon Stock (later St. Simon) at Aylesford, Kent. In this apparition she identified herself as "Our Lady of Mt. Carmel," a name the archangel Michael also used for her during the apparitions at Garabandal in 1961. Mt. Carmel was the ancient site of the Essene Temple (a sect of the Jewish faith at the time of Christ), where, according to the Cayce readings, women served as high-priests. This, of course, would mean that women went into the most sacred place in the Temple, the Holy of Holies, and experienced direct contact with God, returning to give a message to the waiting people. To my knowledge, during this time in history, women were not allowed to enter the Holy of Holies in any of the other Hebrew sects. I don't believe any are doing so today. The Essenes had a rare sense of the Divine Feminine and its representation in woman. The Cayce readings also say that Mary, the mother of Jesus, was trained and chosen at the Temple in Mt. Carmel.

She appears again in 1475 at Bétharram and 1510 at Garaison, both in the Pyrenees Mountains. This is the first of a long and important series of apparitions in the Pyrenees. Note how significant this is when we consider

Cayce's teaching that the great path we have been walking has led from the ancient lands of Atlantis and Egypt to the Death of the Son of Man as a man, then *to the Pyrenees,* and finally to 1998 (see Cayce chapter in this book for details).

Let's focus our attention on six major apparitions, dating from 1531 to 1986: Guadalupe, Lourdes, Fatima, Garabandal, Medjugorje, and Rwanda.

Guadalupe, Mexico, 1531

The Holy Mother's most profound and well-known appearances began at the same time as Nostradramus was divining his quatrains, but faraway from France, in Guadalupe, Mexico, in 1531. She appeared to a native South American Indian. His Indian name in English was "He-who-speaks-like-an-eagle." He and his wife paid taxes to the Aztec governors, but loved the Spanish friars who spoke of one God who was loving, like a father. He and his wife eventually became Christians and changed their names to Juan Diego and Maria Lucia. One hard winter Maria became ill and died. Juan was sad, but believed that Maria was now in heaven with the loving Father. He continued to go to church every Saturday and Sunday.

On December 9, 1531, before dawn, Juan set out for his usual Saturday church devotionals. He was wearing his native Indian clothing, which included a "tilma," a coarse-woven cape made from cactus fiber. As he approached the hill of Tepeyac, he heard what he thought was a choir of birds chanting like the friars. Looking up, he saw a brilliant white cloud upon the hilltop. As he approached the cloud it expanded into a rainbow of color, the chanting stopped, and an exciting silence surrounded the area. Speaking in his own native tongue, a female voice called his name, "Juan, Juan Diego." Without a moment's thought he ran to the top of the hill, the cloud parted, and he saw a beautiful lady in the robes of an Aztec princess. The lady was so brilliant that Juan thought she was standing in front of the Sun but it was before dawn. "Juan, smallest and most believed of my sons," spoke the lady, "Where are you off to, Juanito?" He told her that he was on his way to a special High Mass in honor of the Mother of God. The glowing lady countered, "My dear son, I am the Mother of God, and I want you to listen carefully. I have an important message to give you. Go to the Bishop of Mexico and tell him that I have sent you. Tell him to build a church here because I want to show my love to your people. Tell him all that you have seen."

As one might expect, it was not only difficult to get in to see the Bishop, it was difficult to convince him of the message and the need to build another church in this faraway land. However, the Bishop was not completely resistant to the Indian's story and request, for he instructed Juan to return again another time and repeat the entire story to him. But it had never occurred to Juan that his message would not be received and acted upon immediately. He was in despair as he trudged by the hill of Tepeyac on his way home. To his amazement, the glowing lady was still there! He climbed the hill and said, "Dear lady, I have failed." He told her every detail of his journey and meeting with the Bishop. He closed his story by suggesting that it would be better if she sent a nobleman or a child rather than a poor Indian farmer. She responded, "I have many messengers I could send, but it is you I need and want for this purpose. Go back to the Bishop tomorrow and tell him that *I demand* he build a church here."

As we might expect, the Bishop demanded a sign to prove that she was indeed the Mother of God. Therefore, to prove her authenticity to the Bishop, she imbued Diego's cape with her image. This portrait is still above the altar in the Church of Our Lady of Guadalupe. The fabric of the cape has not aged or changed for over 400 years, even though the cape has been unprotected for much of this time. The paint, if that is what it is, cannot be associated with any that is known.

As far as we know, the glowing lady, "Mother of God," did not prophesy any future events to Juan Diego, except the conversion of his people and her love coming upon them. Furthermore, no one really knows what Guadalupe means. The Lady simply called herself "The Lady of Guadalupe," and so the church became known by this name, but no town or person had ever used the name before. Some researchers have pointed out that the word does have meaning in Arabic—it means: "hidden river." But why she would use an Arabic word is unclear.

After Guadalupe, she appears occasionally, but during the 1800s and the 1900s the frequency and intensity increase dramatically.

In 1830, a vision of the Holy Mother appeared to Catherine Labouré, a nun in a convent in Paris. To Catherine, she prophesied the imminent overthrow of the French throne, very much in keeping with Nostradamus' prophecy of this event. She also told Catherine of events that would occur over the next 40 years. It is claimed that Catherine's body, like Bernadette's of Lourdes, has remained uncorrupted to this day.

Lourdes, France, 1858

In 1846, an apparition of the Holy Mother was reported in LaSalette, France, by a young shepherdess, Agnes de Sagazan, mostly requesting a church be built. But in 1858, one of the greatest and longest-running apparitions occurred in Lourdes, France (continuing the Pyrenees apparitions).

We must remember the times in which these apparitions occurred. In 1793, the French Revolution actually outlawed religion. The parish church in Lourdes had been turned into a gunpowder factory. In the early 1800s, the law was amended and religion was allowed. In 1855, a cholera epidemic broke out in Lourdes and killed many. In 1857-58, famine killed many more in Lourdes. These were very, very hard times.

In the early morning, a fourteen-year-old girl, poor and ill, named Bernadette, was searching among stones and scrubrush for firewood and bones to sell to the rag-and-bone man. She was looking along the river bank when she noticed a glow coming from a small cave in the hillside. The glow was above a rose bush. As she looked closer at this strange sight, she saw a beautiful girl appear, dressed in white. The girl beckoned her to come closer. Bernadette froze in fright and began saying her rosary. The image disappeared. Bernadette told her sister and mother what had happened. Life had been very hard for her mother, and now she believed her eldest daughter was hallucinating! The mother beat Bernadette for "telling stories," and then her sister, too, just to get the point across. The children were forbidden to go near the cave by the river.

Two days later, Bernadette, driven by some inner urge, told her local priest about the whole experience. The priest got her permission to tell the parish priest, Father Peyramale, and the following Sunday, Bernadette received permission to revisit the grotto. Seven girls with holy water approached the cave; Bernadette entered and knelt and prayed. The glowing girl appeared, but only Bernadette could see her. Suddenly, another friend rolled a large stone down the hill from above the cave. The stone landed very close to the cave with a loud crash. Bernadette didn't flinch, remaining entranced. The other girls panicked and ran for help. Finding the local miller, they returned with him to find Bernadette still in trance. He picked her up and carried her back to his mill. Despite his attempts to distract her, she stayed in a focused gaze with a smile on her face. Eventually, she returned to normal, and told everyone what she had seen.

As with so many of the seers of these apparitions, Bernadette was immediately ridiculed and berated. However, some of the townspeople thought Bernadette was truly seeing someone, but it must be, they surmised, the disincarnate soul of a pious girl who had died the year before, rather than the Virgin Mary. One of the prominent women of the town arranged to take Bernadette back to the grotto to observe her and the surroundings during these visions. She put pen and paper in Bernadette's hands and told her to ask the name of the glowing girl and then write it down. Bernadette entered the cave, knelt and prayed. Shortly thereafter, she went into ecstasy. When it was over, Bernadette told them the glowing girl said "it was not necessary to know her name." This was the first time the apparition had spoken, and she spoke in a Pyrenean dialect, Bigourdan, which *Bernadette* knew well, but the prominent lady considered it to be a crude language of the country peasants.

The glowing girl also asked Bernadette to come to the grotto for the next fifteen days, saying, "I don't promise to make you happy in this world, but in the next." During one of these apparitions, Bernadette was observed to be holding a lighted candle while in ecstasy. The candle burned down so low that the flame was actually inside her cupped hands! Yet, when the ecstasy was over, she was found to have suffered no burns. On another occasion, after being in trance during an apparition, Bernadette hugged a sickly child of the town on her way home, and the child became well—for a time. Within the grotto Bernadette was also guided to uncover a healing spring. Unfortunately, when she emerged from her discovery, she was covered with dirt, which the judging crowd saw as demeaning and ridiculous—never realizing how miraculous that spring would prove to pilgrims in the future.

The real story of Lourdes is in its ongoing magic. To date, there have been nearly 4,000 reported cures at this grotto/spring, of which the medical community formally recognizes nearly 200 as inexplicable cures of known illnesses. One of the earliest and most reknowned cures was the healing of the two-year-old son of Napoleon III.

From February 18th to March 4th, Bernadette saw the glowing girl thirteen times, for a total of 18 appearances in all. As far as the prophetic aspect of the apparitions at Lourdes, Bernadette says the glowing girl, who eventually identified herself as "The Immaculate Conception," told her "secrets" of things to come and what she (the glowing girl) was going to do. Little, however, is known about the content of these secrets.

Fatima, Portugal, 1917

"A strong wind began to shake the trees," recalls Lucy, who was nine years old when this happened. "Then, we began to see in the distance, above the trees that stretched to the east, a light whiter than snow, in the form of a young man, quite transparent, and as brilliant as crystal." She and her companions, eight-year-old Francisco and six-year-old Jacinta, watched in wonder as the light being approached them. It said to them, "Do not be afraid. I am the Angel of Peace. Pray with me." They knelt beside him on the bare spot of dirt next to a large white stone, and repeated after him, "My God, I believe, I adore, I hope, and I love You. I ask forgiveness for those who do not believe, nor adore, nor hope, nor love You." Then he was gone.

They returned to their village but told no one of their experience. His coming had left them with a strange feel-

ing of heaviness and portent. In their hearts they won-
dered, and continued that strange prayer.

Later in the summer, he came again, this time to
Lucy's back yard. He asked, "What are you doing? You
must pray! Pray!," explaining to the children that their
prayers could bring peace to Portugal. Lucy, Francisco,
and Jacinta prayed everyday with great intensity and devotion. That fall he came again. This time he came with
the Holy Grail, the Chalice of Communion, which he left
suspended in midair as he knelt with them again to pray.
Rising from prayer, the light being gave the Communion
Host to Lucy, as the body of Christ, and the Chalice to
Jacinta and Francisco, as the blood of Christ. As he did
this he said, "Take and drink the Body and Blood of Jesus
Christ, horribly outraged by ungrateful men. Repair their
crimes and console your God."

When the angel had gone, there was only silence.
None of them spoke. Sealed in this special moment, they
simply sat together in the quiet.

But life goes on, and eventually the children returned
to their normal routines of school, play, and chores. The
following spring, May 13, 1917, to be exact, they were
tending sheep in the pasture, nearly a mile-and-a-half
from home, when it happened again, but with a twist.

At noon, from out of a clear, blue sky came what appeared to be two flashes of lightning. It startled the children. They turned in unison, and above a small holm-oak
tree was the figure of a young lady, about sixteen years
old, all alight, glowing with a sparkling radiance of light.
It appeared that a star was actually wrapped in the folds
of her dress. At first the light seemed too brillant to look
into for long, but the children adjusted to the radiance,
and gradually more details of the lady were visible. She
was wearing a white mantle with gold edges over her
head. Her dress was blue, like the sky. When Lucy asked
who she was, she simply answered "I have come from

heaven." She told the children that she would tell them exactly who she was on October 13th; until then, they were to come to this spot on the 13th of each month and pray. Then she asked, "Will you offer yourselves to God and bear all the sufferings He sends you, in atonement for the sins that offend Him, and for the conversion of sinners?" The children enthusiastically responded, "Oh, we will! We will!" "Then," she said, "you will have a great deal to suffer, but the grace of God will be with you and will strengthen you. Say the rosary everyday to bring peace to the world and an end to war." In a blaze of light, the lady disappeared to the east.

Little Jacinta could not keep silent any longer. The light man, or angel, always filled her with a heavy sense of omen, or something powerful coming. But the light lady filled her with happiness and life. After supper that night, Jacinta told her mother. Little did Jacinta know how the adult world was going to react. Her parents spoke with Francisco's parents, and they all spoke with the parents of the eldest child, Lucy. Lucy's mother was furious and horrified. She believed her daughter had created a terrible hoax, and the whole village would know about it! She beat, begged, and ordered her daughter to recant this disgraceful lie. These were hard times for the children. Reality had raised its powerful head, and there was no room for beings from heaven.

Finally, a month had passed and it was time to return to the site on the 13th of June. The children's parents would not go with them, but some of the villagers came along. To everyone's surprise, the lightning flashed in the midst of the noonday sun and the light lady appeared above the little holm-oak tree. She spoke to the children, saying, "I want you to continue saying the rosary everyday. And after each one of the mysteries, my children, I want you to pray in this way: 'O my Jesus, forgive us and deliver us from the fire of hell. Take all souls to heaven, especially those in greatest need.'" Lucy, perhaps weary of the earth's harsh reaction to her claims of heavenly visions, asked the Lady, "Will you take us to heaven?" Surprisingly, the Lady answered, "Yes. I will take Jacinta and Francisco soon, but you will remain a little longer, since Jesus wishes you to make me known and loved on earth. He wishes also for you to establish devotion in the world to my Immaculate Heart."

The crowd who knelt around the children saw the lightning, but not the apparition. However, they could hear a small voice speaking in response to Lucy's comments and questions, but could not make out what it was saying. Above the tree, they saw only a little cloud. When Lucy said the Lady was leaving, the crowd saw the little cloud rise very slowly and move off to the east. This, however, was enough phenomena to make the children celebrities. Unfortunately, to some people, they were notorious celebrities of the ridiculous! Strangers and neighbors began to ridicule and taunt the children. People in authority questioned them over and over for every weary detail, looking for the flaw in their stories. Lucy's mother and the local priest had almost convinced Lucy that she had been duped by the Devil! The little girl was in torment over the whole thing. It was as the light Lady had foretold, the children suffered much for what they had seen. Lucy had actually decided not to go on the 13th of the next month.

On July 13th, the village of Fatima was shocked when hundreds of seekers from all over came to their village to join with the children in the vigil for the Lady of Light. It was a hot summer day. The sun was blinding. However, at noon, the sun paled, though the sky was cloudless and blue. Silence swept through the crowds as they began to hear "a little buzzing sound." Many saw a little ball of light settle above the tiny holm-oak tree. But the sight of the Lady and the sound of her voice were only seen and heard by the children. Not surprisingly, Lucy came at the last minute, driven by something inside of her, despite all the terrible repercussions that were sure to follow.

The Lady repeated her request for prayer to end war and bring peace to the world, and promised that she would reveal her identify on October 13th. She gave another prayer, "O Jesus, this is for the love of thee, for the conversion of sinners, and in reparation for sins committed against the Immaculate Heart of Mary." Then, she told the children a threefold secret. This was followed by a view into the nature of Hell, which the Lady sadly said, "Where the souls of sinners go. It is to save them that God wants to establish in the world devotion to my Immaculate Heart. If you do what I tell you, many souls will be saved, and there will be peace." Then followed a prophecy of the fate of humanity and of nations from 1917 into the future. With a clap of thunder the vision was over.

The crowd pressed in upon the children, some seeking to touch their garments, some to spit into their little faces and mock them. The cruelty of the unbelievers was surprising. Lucy's mother beat her with a broom stick. Every woman in the village deemed it their duty to slap sense into these crazy, trouble-making children. These little ones could go nowhere without physical and emotional abuse and torment.

On the 13th of September, the children were much weary of the world's oppressive reaction to their visions of heaven and light beings. They had suffered at the hands of cruel, condemning people, even among their own loved ones. When the Lady appeared that month, Lucy began with this pleading request, "So many believe that I am an impostor and a cheat that they say I deserve to be hanged and burned. Will you please perform a miracle so that all of them can believe?" Just as Jesus was always asked to show the doubters a sign, so little Lucy was now asking the Lady to show her a sign. When the Lady agreed to show all a sign on October 13th, the children proclaimed it openly, believing that everyone would begin to act differently. To their surprise, the ridicule and abuse increased. As the date approached, the newspapers were printing satirical stories about "the three little deceivers." Freemason groups and civic groups threatened to bomb the children's homes. In the night, Lucy's distraught mother would wake her from sleep, shaking her and demanding that she confess her fantasy before it was too late.

Finally, October 13th arrived. Seventy thousand people crammed into the pasture to witness the event! Some came to see the farce, others to witness a miracle from God. It was bitter cold. Rain fell all night and into the day. Thousands of black umbrellas created an eerie scene across the pasture. Many prayed and chanted. The rain grew intense. Gray, wet and cold was the aura of that day. Exactly at noon, the children fell to their knees, with chins turned upward, rain pouring onto their faces. They were obviously looking at and listening to something. Throughout the vision Mary prophesied things to come and instructions that must be followed. In the vision she identified herself as had been promised back on May 13th, saying, "I am the Lady of the Rosary," which of course we know is Mary (most of the beads on a rosary are for the prayer, "Hail Mary").

Our focus here is on the prophecies that Mother Mary delivered at Fatima and many other places and times throughout this century. To the Fatima children she confided the following:

The Prophecies of Fatima

1. Evil, sin and hell-like torment do indeed exist, despite the fashionable ideas to the contrary. Evildoers, sinners, abiders in hell, and lost souls must soon begin

to turn from their ways and catch hold of God's light and love, before it is too late. The children felt an ominous implication in all of this—something is going to happen, and it's going to happen soon. Everyone had better get their house in order and their hearts right with God. Also, all seekers of God should pray for the conversion of evil and lost souls.

2. World War I will end within one year if you pray for peace and an end to war (spoken on October 13, 1917). WWI ended with the signing of an armistice on November 11, 1918.

3. The "war that was to end all wars" (WWI) would be followed by an even worse war. The evil of this war would be preceded by a great light in the sky, which many in Europe saw. She also said the war would occur during the reign of a Pope named "Pius XI" (specifically named by the Lady). At the time of this prophecy, the reigning Pope was Benedict XV. WWII began in 1936, during the reign of Pius XI.

4. In 1917 the Lady prophesied that a great battle for the heart of Russia was engaged. At this time in history, Russia was still a strong religious country, mostly Eastern Orthodox Catholic. The Lady said, "If Russia consecrates herself to the Immaculate Heart, then there will be peace. If not, then Russia will spread her errors throughout the world, bringing new wars and persecution... Certain nations will be annihilated." All of us who have the benefit of hindsight know that Russia became the Soviet Union, gobbling up nations and peoples everywhere. Bolshevik-style Communism became the dark banner under which she travelled the world, creating her "Soviet Bloc." In 1917, Communism was simply a theory, not a threat, but the Bolshevik revolution was taking

place in 1917. Little did the world know how powerful and menacing Bolshevik Communism would become in future decades, right up until the fall of the Soviet Union in the 1980s. Here in the 90s, religion is making a come-back in a broken and struggling Russia, and nations that had been gobbled up in the Union of Soviet Socialist Republic, are once again independent.

Garabandal, Spain, 1961

The entry for June 18, 1961, in 13-year-old Maria Concepcion Gonzalez's (nicknamed Conchita) diary reads as follows:

> Suddenly, there appeared to me a very beautiful figure that shone brilliantly but did not hurt my eyes at all. When the other three girls—Jacinta, Loli, and Mari Cruz—saw me in this state of ecstasy, they thought that I was having a fit, because I kept saying, with my hands clasped: "Ay! Ay! Oh! Oh!" They were about to call my mother when they found themselves in the same state as I, and cried out together: "Ay! Oh! The angel!"
>
> There was a short silence among the four of us. Then, all of a sudden the angel disappeared and we returned to normal. Greatly frightened, we ran toward the church. As we passed the dance that was going on in the village, a girl named Pili Gonzalez said to us, "You look pale and scared!" We said together, "It is because we have seen an angel!" "Is it true?" she asked. We said together, "Yes, yes!"
>
> Then we continued on in the direction of the church. When we arrived at the church, we went around back and cried. Some little girls playing there asked, "Why are you crying?" We

said, "Because we saw an angel." They ran off to tell the schoolmistress.

When we stopped crying, we went into the church. The schoolmistress arrived in a very frightened state and asked us, "Is it true that you have seen an angel?" We simply replied, "Yes, yes." She then led us on a station [this is the Stations of the Cross, a series of prayers before pictures of the various stages Jesus went through in his arrest, scourging, crucifixion, death and resurrection], giving thanks to Jesus in the Blessed Sacrament.

When we finished the station, we all went home. My mother wanted me home before dark, but it was now nine o'clock and dark. She said, "Haven't I told you that you should get home while it is still daylight?"

I was very upset by these two things—having seen such a beautiful figure and having arrived home late. I don't dare go into the kitchen. I lean up against the door post and say, "I've seen an angel."

Mother says, "Coming home late, you come in here and tell me things like that!"

"But I did see an angel!"

We didn't say anything more about the matter that evening. The rest of the time was spent in the usual manner without talking about anything at all.

But the next day would prove to be a different situation. The word had spread all over town—four hysterical girls had run to the church crying because they had seen something. Now, the questioning and ridicule was to begin. Much of it occurred on the way to school by older children and adults. Once in school, however, their peers were very interested in all the details. School let out at one o'clock, and on their way home the town pastor caught up with them. He believed that they might have made a mistake in their assumption that it was an angel. Separating Conchita from the other children, he demanded that she be honest about this whole thing. But there was a nervousness about the priest that caused Conchita to recite every moment and detail of the event to him carefully. She noticed how attentively he listened. When she was done, he demanded that she ask the angel-like being to identify himself—that is, if he came again.

The pastor questioned each of the other children separately as he had Conchita. It was obvious to all that he was becoming more certain the children had seen something special. But he told everyone that he would wait to see if any more appearances occurred before he told the bishop.

The next days went by as most other days. Except for the visitors and the questions, life was normal—school, play, and meals—until the girls desired to return to the spot. This caused their families to get upset. The overall feeling was to stay away from trouble; don't go looking for it. Conchita's mother started crying about "the mess." Life had been going just fine until this angel stuff. Conchita writes in her diary that she asked her mother to suppose it was true. "What then?" she asked. This reflection caused her mother to let her go.

Conchita called the spot "a corner of heaven" (un trocito de cielo). But on their way, the people made fun of them, asking "Why don't you go to the church to pray rather than that alley?" Some of the people actually tried to chase the children away, but they would not go. Then, as the children prayed, others began throwing stones at them. The children endured this, continuing to pray. After a long time, it became evident that the angel wasn't coming. As the children walked home, the schoolmistress met them and asked if they had been to the alley. When they explained that they had and that nothing had happened, she responded, as though it was common knowledge, that the angel didn't come because it was very cloudy!

As the days passed without another appearance, more and more people began to think that it had all been the children's imagination—even the children themselves were beginning to wonder.

The original appearance had occurred at about 8:30 p.m., but since it was summer, it was still light. On the evening of the 20th of June, the children happened to get together again. So they decided to try again. In the alley they prayed their rosary and then, as they were leaving for their homes, a bright light began to shine. It was so bright that the children could no longer see each other. Unfortunately, they became frightened and began to scream. The brilliant light disappeared.

The next day, the children tried again. This time when the angel appeared, the children remained calm. They even asked him who he was and why he had come. He did not answer. The appearance was over shortly. But everyone watching the girls was now convinced that they were seeing something very special.

The evening of the 22nd, near the usual time, 8:30 p.m., the angel appeared again. The surrounding people only saw the children go into ecstasy. No other phenomena were seen by them. However, the expression on the children's faces caused an excitement to spread through the crowd, and the people began to shout, *Era cierto!*, "It's true!"

As usual, the crowds attracted the police, and the police began to look for causes beyond the heavenly ones. Hypnosis was suspected and a charge was made against these girls and a man of the town who had been at the scene and who knew and practiced hypnosis. They wanted to put him in jail. But so many in the crowd were convinced that it was not hypnosis and testified that the man had nothing to do with the children before or during the appearance that the police took no action.

During the next appearance, which was a little earlier in the evening, many of the authorities were present. Their disbelief caused them to do many cruel things to these children. Conchita's own doctor lifted her up during the ecstasy (she was in a kneeling position) and dropped her from a height of 3 feet onto the stone street to see if she was faking it. There was a noise like cracking bones that caused many onlookers to cringe. Her legs remained bent in the kneeling position throughout the incident, and she landed on her knees. She was obviously not aware of what had just happened to her and remained in her ecstatic state. When she returned to normal consciousness, some concerned ladies began to examine and care for her knees.

Afterward, the authorities took the children to the church, isolated them, and began to interrogate them.

On the 26th and 27th, word had spread far and wide, and many people came to witness the angelic appearance. However, nothing happened. Disillusionment filled the crowd and the children. The believers were disappointed and the nonbelievers were filled with the pride of their certainty about things like this. Conchita remembers thinking, "If God wants it that way, that is the way it must be."

On the 28th, the angel appeared again, but this time at nine o'clock, and the ecstasy lasted until 10 o'clock. The angel was very happy at the faith and persistence of the children and their supporters, but did not say this or anything else. The children could simply sense his feelings. He appeared again and again over the next few days, until July 1, when he finally spoke.

"Do you know why I have come?" the angel asked. "It is to announce to you that tomorrow, Sunday, the Virgin Mary will appear to you as Our Lady of Mount Carmel." The children replied, "We hope she comes soon!" The angel only smiled. Then the angel spoke with the children for two hours, which seemed like only a few minutes to the children.

Much of the conversation was friendly and casual, with the angel asking them if they remembered how concerned they had become when first they saw Conchita "have a fit" and were going to go get her mother? The children told the angel it was because she looked so strange. Then they all, including the angel, laughed. Finally, the angel said he would return tomorrow with the "Blessed Virgin."

Unlike the children's experiences at Fatima, the appearances of the angel at Garabandal caused the children great joy and uplifting. You'll recall the Fatima children, especially the youngest, felt great foreboding when in the presence of the angel. The Garabandal children only felt a great sadness after he had disappeared, wishing they could stay in his presence always.

During this appearance, the children noticed "a sign" that they had also seen in one of the previous appearances. Below the angel was a banner. On it were some words and below them were some Roman numerals:

It is necessary that
XVII-MCMLXI

In the previous appearance, the children simply did not want to take their eyes off the angel long enough to clearly see the banner. But in this appearance, they had plenty of time. They even asked the angel what it meant, to which he replied that the Virgin would tell them.

During this appearance the children also discerned

more details of the angel's features and clothing. In her diary, Conchita describes him as follows:

> The angel was dressed in a long, flowing, blue garment without a belt. His wings were pale rose, long, and very lovely. His little face was not long or round. His nose was very pretty. His eyes black and his skin dark. His hands were very delicate and his fingernails short. We did not see his feet.

On Sunday, July 2, 1961, the town was packed with people from all over. From the church, the girls and the crowd headed for the alley, but never made it. Along the way, around 6 p.m., the Blessed Virgin appeared with an angel on each side of her. One of them was Michael the archangel, whom the children knew. The other angel they did not recognize, but he was dressed exactly like Michael. The children thought they looked like twins. Next to the unknown angel was a large eye, which the children thought was the eye of God.

Conchita's dairy describes the Lady this way:

> The Blessed Virgin appeared in a white dress, a blue mantle with a crown of small golden stars above her head. Her feet were not visible. Her hands were wide open. Her hair is long, dark brown and wavy, and parted in the middle. She has an oval shaped face and her nose is long and delicate. Her mouth is very pretty with rather full lips. The color of her face is dark, but lighter than the angel's—it's different. Her voice is very lovely, a very unusual voice that I can't describe. There is no woman that resembles the Blessed Virgin in her voice, or anything else. In her arms she sometimes

carries the baby Jesus. He is very tiny, like a newborn with a little face. His complexion is like that of the Blessed Virgin's.

From this apparition on, everyone close to the girls, including most of the townspeople and the pastor, believed and supported them. Their parents actually began to prepare and remind the children that the hour (6 p.m.) was approaching and they should get to the spot and begin praying. However, the children began to realize that in the past they always were "called" to come to the site. This was a surprise to everyone. The children explained that they "heard" an inner voice, but not with their ears, nor were their names actually called. In fact, there were three types of calling! One was a feeling of joy stirring within them. Another was stronger, with a noticeable sense of excitement rising within them. And the final and most powerful calling was a full, almost overwhelming feeling of excitement and happiness. The children said that they usually departed for the site on the second calling.

Not surprisingly, when the girls had finished describing the calls, they got a call! As is so common, the adult doubters still tried to test the girls. They came up with a plan to separate the girls in different homes, and then see if all four got the "calling" at the same time. A half-hour after being separated, all four girls got the second calling at the same time and arrived at the new site of the apparitions at the same time. This really did amaze many of the doubters.

As soon as they arrived, the apparition occurred. It was 7 p.m. The Holy Mother had the baby Jesus in her arms, but the angels were nowhere to be seen. Some of the people who had come with the children had given them objects for the Blessed Mother to kiss, and she kissed all of them. They asked to hold the baby Jesus, but both the baby and Mother only smiled at the request. She disappeared saying, "Tomorrow, you will see me again."

The kissed objects had the sweet scent of perfume about them. Everyone was excited. During the apparition, the observers saw the girls playing with what appeared to be a baby, but they didn't actually see the baby.

It is interesting to note that the Garabandal girls never mentioned in their statements or journals any bright light or luminosity around the Blessed Mother. She appeared with clear form to her. However, the children do say that though she kissed them good-bye, they never really felt a physical contact to their heads, and when holding the baby they felt pressure but not physical contact. It was not a physical presence, or body, yet everything else about it seemed real.

On October 18th, we receive the first message from the Blessed Mother. Actually, the message was given to the children on July 4th, but they were to reveal it publicly after the apparition on the 18th of October.

She begins by asking them if they knew what the sign meant that the angel revealed to them. She told them it meant that, "We must make many sacrifices, perform much penance, and visit the Blessed Sacrament [communion] frequently. But first, we must lead good lives. If we do not, a chastisement will befall us. The cup is already filling up and if we do not change, a very great chastisement will come upon us."

After this apparition, the children wrote the message and signed it. All agreed that this was exactly what the Blessed Mother said. The children added, "The Blessed Virgin wants us to do these things, so that we may avoid God's punishment."

The Garabandal apparitions are many. They began in June 1961 and continued until November 1965. Throughout the recorded experiences and messages, there are prophecies. The first is about this "chastisement." The second is a "warning " (el aviso). And, the third is a "miracle"—Conchita was the only one to receive the miracle information and is to announce its coming eight days prior to the event.

The Miracle

By this time, many authorities were asking for a sign, a miracle. When the children asked the Blessed Mother to perform one for the doubters, she turned very grave and stopped smiling. Once, when a tape recorder had been brought to the scene, the children pleaded with Her to speak onto the tape. Just as they were waiting for her to speak, the tape ran out, then an audible voice that everyone heard said, "I will not speak."

The miracle she prophesied is to occur in such a manner that the whole world will know it. Here is how Conchita describes it:

> I am the only one to whom the Blessed Virgin spoke of the miracle. She forbade me to say what it will consist of. I can't announce the date either until eight days before it is due to occur. What I can reveal is that it will coincide with an event in the Church and with the feast of a saint, martyr of the Eucharist; that it will take place at eight-thirty on a Thursday evening; that it will be visible to all those who are in the village and surrounding mountains; that the sick who are present will be cured and the doubters will believe. It will be the greatest miracle that Jesus has performed for the world. There won't be the slightest doubt that it comes from God and that it is for the good of mankind. A sign of the miracle (un senal del milagro), which it will be possible to film or

televise, will remain forever (para seimpre) at the pines.

After reading Nostradamus' prophecy of Thursday becoming a Holy Day, Conchita's Thursday miracle is interesting. Could this miracle be the beginning of a new leader whose Holy Day will be recognized as Thursday because a great miracle occurred on that day, at 8:30 p.m.? Certainly, if it is to be "the greatest miracle that Jesus has performed for the world," it's going to be a doozy, deserving of a special Holy Day. I thought raising Lazarus was a pretty good miracle. Of course, only a few dozen people saw that one.

When Conchita was asked to explain more about the sign that will remain at the Pines (an area in Garabandal where many apparitions took place), she said:

> The sign that will remain forever at the pines is something that we will be able to photograph, televise and see, but not touch. It will be evident that it is not a thing of this world but from God.

As of yet, Conchita has not gotten the message to alert us eight days before the miracle occurs.

The Chastisement
Conchita explains the chastisement this way:

> The chastisement is conditional and depends on whether or not mankind heeds the messages of the Blessed Virgin and the miracle. If it should take place, I know what it will consist of because the Blessed Virgin told me about it, but I am not permitted to say what it is. Moreover, I have *seen* the chastisement. I

can assure you that if it comes, it is worse than being enveloped in fire [Van Allen Belts again?], worse than having fire above and beneath you. I do not know how much time will elapse between the miracle and the chastisement.

If we do not change, the chastisement will be terrible in keeping with what we deserve. We saw it, but I cannot say what it consists of because I do not have permission from the Blessed Virgin to do so. I cannot say anything else about the chastisement. When I saw it, I felt a very great fear even though I was looking at the Blessed Virgin.

Interestingly, while the children were viewing the chastisement, many onlookers noticed how terrified they were, and began to pray. As soon as they did so, the children's cries and anguish subsided. But as soon as the onlookers stopped praying, the children immediately went into crying and squirming as though suffering great discomfort.

The Warning

Conchita wrote that when the world sees the warning, the people will wish that they were dead rather than experience it. She goes on to say:

The Blessed Virgin told me on the first of January that a warning would be given before the miracle so that the world might amend itself. This warning, like the chastisement, is a very fearful thing for the good as well as for the wicked. It will draw the good closer to God and it will warn the wicked that the end of time is coming and that these are the last warnings. There is more to it than this, but it can't be said by letter. No one can stop it from happening. It is certain, although I know nothing concerning the day or the date.

Along with her statement, Conchita answered specific questions. Of the 18 questions submitted to Conchita on September 14, 1965, four relate to the warning.

Q. Will the warning be a visible thing or an interior thing or both?

A. The warning is a thing that comes directly from God and will be visible throughout the entire world, in whatever place anyone might be.

Q. Will the warning reveal his personal sins to every person in the world and to persons of all faiths, including atheists?

A. Yes, the warning will be like a revelation of our sins, and it will be seen and experienced equally by believers and nonbelievers and people of any religion whatsoever.

Q. Is it true that the warning will cause many people to remember the dead?

A. The warning is like a purification for the miracle. And it is a sort of a catastrophe. It will make us think of the dead, that is, we would prefer to be dead than to experience the warning.

Q. Will the warning be recognized and accepted by the world as a direct sign from God?

A. Certainly, and for this reason I believe it is impossible that the world could be so hardened as not to change.

Finally, Conchita says that the Blessed Mother told her that there would only be two more Popes after Paul VI!

Here are Conchita's own words on this:

> The Blessed Virgin said in 1962 that there
> will be only two more Popes after Paul VI. But
> this does not mean that the world will come to
> an end.

Now we all know the Papal prophecies of Malacy, the
Monk of Padua, and Nostradamus' from previous chapters. This Garabandal prophecy does not seem to fit with
these other prophecies of Papal succession. The Popes
during the Garabandal apparitions were John XXIII
(1958-63) and then Paul VI (1963-78). Using Conchita's
statement, the current Pope, John Paul II, would then be
the last Pope. Whereas, Malachy, the Monk of Padua and
Nostradamus foresaw two more Popes after the current
one. We shall see.

Medjugorje, Yugoslavia, 1981

These apparitions begin in a similar manner to those
in Fatima and Garabandal. A 17-year-old girl sees a luminous silhouette suspended above the ground on a
cloud, and calls to her girlfriends, "Look, there's Our
Lady, the Blessed Mother." Six children are involved in
these apparitions, 2 boys and 4 girls. Most are 16 and 17
years old, but one is only 10. Most of the apparitions occur on or around a mountain, Mt. Podbrodo. As with
other apparitions, the children see many wonders, encounter many stern and accusing adults and authorities,
but endure to convince many of their sincerity. Onlookers also see miraculous phenomena, which helps to support the belief that something special was happening.

Basically, the luminous lady identifies herself as "The
Mother of Peace," and explains:

> I have come to tell the world that God is

truth; He exists. True happiness and the full-
ness of life are in Him. I have come here as
Queen of Peace to tell the world that peace is
necessary for the salvation of the world. In
God, one finds true joy from which true peace
is derived.

At another time she says, "I have come because there
are many believers here. I want to be with you to convert
and reconcile everyone."
She explains:

You know that I wish to guide you on the way
of holiness, but I do not want to force you. I do
not want you to be holy by force. I wish every
one of you to help yourselves and me by your
little sacrifices, so that I can guide you to be
more holy, day by day. Therefore, dear children, I do not want to force you to live the messages; but rather, this long time I am with you
shows that I love you immeasureably and that
I wish every single one of you to be holy.

The Chastisement

The Queen of Peace gives the Medjugorje children 10
"secrets." The children were told not to reveal the secrets
until she gave them permission. It is known that some of
the secrets deal with a chastisement that will come to
the world. There is some uncertainty about whether this
chastisement has already been averted or is yet to come.
Apparently, the 7th secret prophesied a chastisement,
but the 8th secret said that the chastisement had already
been avoided because of world prayer. However, the 9th
and 10th secrets each include chastisements. Now,
whether these are new chastisements or the same as
those mentioned in the 7th secret is unclear to some

writers. As I read the material, it appears they are new and different chastisements which are still to come. Perhaps one or both of them correspond with the chastisement the children saw at Garabandal.

Whatever the case, the Queen says that this chastisement can be mitigated "through prayer and fasting." She teaches that the world has lost its understanding of the value of prayer and fasting, and that much can be changed by these practices. She explains:

> Pray with great meditation. Do not look at your watch all the time, but allow yourself to be led by the grace of God. Do not concern yourself too much with the things of this world, but entrust all that in prayer to Our Heavenly Father . . . Avoid television . . . excessive sports, the unreasonable enjoyment of food and drink, alcohol, tobacco . . . Definitely eliminate all anguish. Whoever abandons himself to God does not have room in his heart for anguish.

She encourages having "an encounter with God in prayer," a "meeting with God, the Creator." She says, "God gives Himself to you but He wants you to answer in your own freedom to His invitation."

The Sign

Another secret deals with a sign, a sign left by the Queen that the whole world will see. The children all claim to know when the sign or event is to occur. The sign is to appear on the apparitional hill. Its presence will be a call for mankind to return to God. "The Virgin said that there would be many more signs throughout the world before the great sign appears." But after the great sign appears, there will be no more time for "conversion." That is why the Virgin calls all to reconcile themselves with God now.

The Warning

Before the visible sign is given, there will come three warnings to the world in the form of singular events on Earth "to allow people to return to God." Once the warnings begin, they will follow in short succession to one another. Enough time will pass between them to allow people to become sufficiently aware of each warning. During this period, many graces will pour out upon the people who seek attunement to God. This is reminiscent of many biblical prophecies:

> Isa. 44:3 For I will pour water on the thirsty land, and streams on the dry ground; I will pour out my Spirit on your offspring, and my blessing on your descendants.

> Ezek. 39:29 I will no longer hide my face from them, for I will pour out my Spirit on the house of Israel, declares the Sovereign LORD."

> Joel 2:28 And afterward, I will pour out my Spirit on all people. Your sons and daughters will prophesy, your old men will dream dreams, your young men will see visions.
> Joel 2:29 Even on my servants, both men and women, I will pour out my Spirit in those days.

> Acts 2:17 In the last days, God says, I will pour out my Spirit on all people. Your sons and daughters will prophesy, your young men will see visions, your old men will dream dreams.
> Acts 2:18 Even on my servants, both men and women, I will pour out my Spirit in those

days, and they will prophesy.

The Guidance

Throughout the Medjugorje apparitions, the Queen gives much guidance as to what one should be doing in these times. Here are two examples:

> Try to conquer some fault. If your fault is to get angry at everything, try each day to get angry less . . . If you cannot stand those who do not please you, try on a given day to speak with them. If your fault is not to be able to stand an arrogant person, you should try to approach that person. If you desire that person to be humble, be humble yourselves. Show that humility is worth more than pride.
>
> You yourselves know what you have to do. Make a decision for love. Love your neighbors. Love those people from whom the evil is coming to you and so . . . you will be able to judge the intentions of the heart. In the power of love you can do even those things that seem impossible to you . . . Hatred creates division and does not see anybody or anything. Carry unity and peace. Act with love in the place where you live. Let love always be your only tool. With love turn everything to good.

There is also a universality about the teachings from the Queen of Peace. As in this teaching:

> You must respect each man's beliefs. No one should despise another for his convictions. God is one and invisible. It is not God but believers who have caused the dreadful divisions in the world.

Mirjana, one of the six children, tells of being taught by the Lady that devout Roman Catholics go out of their way to avoid contact with Orthodox Catholics and Muslims; yet nobody who refused to take other believers seriously was worthy of the name of Christian. The Lady singled out one of Mirjana's neighbors in Sarajevo, a Muslim woman called Pasha. "She is a true believer, a saintly woman. You should try to be more like her."

As all of us now know, peace did not come to Sarajevo. The dark influence prevailed and the people chose "ethnic cleansing" rather than cooperation, understanding, and love.

Rwanda, Africa, 1981

Two rival tribes have been fighting in this little country since 1959, leading to a civil war in 1990. A year before the apparitions began, pictures, statues, and other icons of the Virgin Mother were stolen, damaged, or destroyed in an iconoclasm that distressed many of the faithful, who cried and prayed to heaven for relief from this terror. It is thought that this may have caused the apparitions to begin in 1981.

Seven young people, from ages 16 to 21, experienced visions of the Blessed Mother *separately*, each seeing her personally, never as a group. The visions lasted an hour or more, during which time the voice of the visionary was amplified somehow for the listening crowd to better hear—all in the native language of the Rwandans. Four of the young people were in a girls' boarding school. It was run by Rwandan Catholic nuns caring for children of any religion. In the following year ('82), the Blessed Mother appeared and spoke to five other girls from January to August. By December of '82 only a 16-year-old girl, Alphonsine, was still having visions. She continued to see the apparitions until January of 1986! However, in 1989, on the anniversary of the first apparition, November 28th, Alphonsine saw the Blessed Mother one more time. The divine image told her that there would be no more appearances.

During these many apparitions, the image identified herself as "The Mother of the Word." This is a powerful title, referencing St. John's opening lines to his gospel:

> John 1:1-5 In the beginning was the Word, and the Word was with God, and the Word was God. This One was with God in the beginning. Through this One all things were made; without this One nothing was made that has been made. In this One was life, and that life was the light of men. The light shines in the darkness, but the darkness has not understood it.

Normally, "this One" is translated "Him," but the original Greek is "this One." As we have discussed in the chapter of Biblical Prophecies, "Word" is the English translation for the Greek word "logos." Logos means much more than word. It is the essence of beingness, all consciousness. In Luke 21:33 Jesus uses "logos" once again when he says, "Heaven and earth will pass away, but my word will never pass away."

"The Mother of the Word" is calling us to attune ourselves to the Word, the Logos, and prepare for coming changes.

During the 1990s, apparitions have diminished, but messages from the Holy Mother still come. Many claim to be having "inner locutions," a term used to describe the hearing of a distinctive voice within ones consciousness—in these cases, it is the voice of the Holy Mother. Others describe their Marian messages as coming by means of psychic channeling. Whatever the means, the message still seems to be the same.

One recently popular book is Annie Kirkwood's *Mary's*

Message to the World. In this book, Mrs. Kirkwood says she "takes dictation from Mary," hearing her thoughts and then writing them on a computer word processor. Here is an example of one of Mrs. Kirkwood's inner messages from Mary:

> Make sure you understand that this is not the end, but the beginning of a new era and a new world and a new understanding. The need to prepare is now, right before the birth of this new era.

All the apparitions of the Holy Mother require some degree of faith on the part of those seeking to understand what it's all about and whether it really is Mary, the mother of Jesus. The parish priest at Lourdes, Father Dominique Peyramale, said, "For those who believe no explanation is necessary. For those who do not believe, no explanation is possible." Maybe, but I'd like to attempt an explanation, or at least some elaboration.

The Divine Feminine

The most important element of this is a greater understanding of the entity involved. Who is this entity and what is her role in the big picture?

The Essenes believed that God is both male and female in one, and that the Logos, the essence of being, is in this same image. Therefore, to them, there is a Divine Masculine and a Divine Feminine.

The Essenes believed that God meant what He said when He turned to Eve as they were leaving the Garden and prophesied that out of her would come the redeemer of this fall from grace. Therefore, the Essenes were preparing for the coming of the Messiah by looking for the "Eve" that would deliver Him. They knew that the Logos and the original Adam were male and female in one. It was only later that they were separated into Adam and Eve. Therefore, to the Essenes, the Messiah had to have a feminine component, and God had foreshadowed this in His prophecy.

There were several females in their Mt. Carmel temple that the Essenes thought might be chosen to fulfill Eve's destiny. One day, a lady named Anne came to their temple. She told them that she was pregnant, but had not known any man. This was exactly what they had been looking for! In fact, some in the temple had actually considered Anne to be the female component of the coming of the Messiah. However, when she delivered a female child, some began to believe that even the feminine component had to be immaculately conceived since it was half of the Logos. Mary proved to be just that. While still very young and before she was married to Joseph, she conceived the Holy Child. Here's how Luke records their conversation:

> Luke 1:26-42 In the sixth month, God sent the angel Gabriel to Nazareth, a town in Galilee, to a virgin pledged to be married to a man named Joseph, a descendant of David. The virgin's name was Mary.
>
> And coming in to her the angel said, "Hail O woman richly blessed! The Lord is with you." Mary was greatly troubled at his words, and kept pondering what manner of greeting this might be.
>
> But the angel said to her, "Do not be afraid, Mary, you have found favor with God. Behold, you will conceive in your womb and give birth to a son, and you are to give him the name Jesus. He will be great and will be called the Son of the Most High. The Lord God will give him the throne of his father David, and he will

reign over the house of Jacob forever; his kingdom will never end."

"How will this be," Mary asked the angel, "since I am a virgin?"

The angel answered, "The Holy Spirit will come upon you, and the power of the Most High will overshadow you; for that reason the holy one to be born will be called the Son of God. Even Elizabeth, your relative, is going to have a child in her old age, and she who was said to be barren is in her sixth month. For nothing is impossible with God."

"Behold, I am the servant of the Lord," Mary answered. "May it be done to me as you have said."

Then the angel left her.

At that time Mary got ready and hurried to a town in the hill country of Judea, where she entered Zechariah's home and greeted Elizabeth. When Elizabeth heard Mary's greeting, the baby leaped in her womb, and Elizabeth was filled with the Holy Spirit. She cried out with a loud voice, "Blessed among women are you, and blessed is the fruit of your womb!"

What wonderful and powerful scenes. For the Essenes, the key insight comes in one of the verses that follows these. Elizabeth, filled with the Holy Spirit, speaks the prophecy that the Essenes had held to so faithfully.

Blessed is she who believed that there would be fulfillment of what had been spoken to her by the Lord. (Luke 1:45)

"Fulfillment of what had been spoken to her by the Lord," spoken when? To the Essenes, it was when they were leaving the Garden. Out of Eve would come the re-deemer of this fall from grace. In Mary, the Holy Mother, this prophecy was fulfilled.

The Divine Feminine was prophesied to precede the coming of the Divine Masculine, and it did so. Perhaps the Holy Mother's apparitions are in sync with a pattern. Perhaps this means that He will follow soon.

Notes

Chapter 1

1. See *A Commentary on the Revelation,* Edgar Cayce, published by A.R.E. Press.
2. See *After the End of Time: Revelation and the Growth of Consciousness,* Robin Robertson, Ph.D., Inner Vision Publishing.
3. See Matt. 4.
4. Heb. 2.
5. Matt. 22:21.
6. Matt. 17:26-27.
7. John 15:13.
8. See also Psalm 37:7.
9. 1 Kings 6:1.
10. 2 Kings 25:8.
11. Ezra 3.
12. ICor. 15:52.
13. In Greek, it would be Christos or Christ. Messiah and Christos both mean "Anointed One."

Chapter 2

1. Their address and phone number are: A.R.E., P.O. Box 595, 67th St. and Atlantic Ave., Virginia Beach, VA 23451-0595, (757) 428-3588.
2. This is a clear reference to Jesus' comments in Matthew 24.

Chapter 3

1. See Cayce reading 281-33 for one example; there are many others.
2. The first number refers to the Century and the second to the quatrain.

3.　Brennan, J.H., N*ostramdamus: Visions and the Future*, 1992, Aquarian Press, London, p. 95.

4.　*Ibid*, p. 100.

5.　Matt. 24:12.

6.　Roberts, Henry C., *The Complete Prophecies of Nostradamus*, 1947, Nostradamus Company, Osterbay, N.Y., p. 335.

7.　Readings 294-151

8.　For more on this story read John Cornwell's *A Thief in the Night.*

9.　See Rev. 20:7.

10.　Reading 5748-6.

11.　See Matt. 24:35.

12.　More on this in Chapter One.

13.　See Matt. 24:19.

A.R.E. PRESS

The A.R.E. Press publishes books, videos, and audiotapes meant to improve the quality of our readers' lives—personally, professionally, and spiritually. We hope our products support your endeavors to realize your career potential, to enhance your relationships, to improve your health, and to encourage you to make the changes necessary to live a loving, joyful, and fulfilling life.

For more information or to receive a free catalog, call:

1-800-723-1112

Or write:

A.R.E. Press
215 67th Street
Virginia Beach, VA 23451-2061